The Great Exchange

Bound by Blood

By

Robert C. Camenisch

and

Kay W. Camenisch

Cover design by Daniel D. Camenisch

ISBN 978-1-942587-05-7

Visit the authors' website at www.randkcamenisch.com.

Table of Contents

Dedication

This book is dedicated to Reichardt and Elizabeth Taylor, missionaries to Brazil from 1947 to 1983. They introduced us to a deeper understanding of the ancient ritual of blood covenant and its implications for our lives as Christians. Reichardt and Elizabeth were people of prayer who prayed for us every day as long as they lived. We are grateful for their impact in our lives.

"Oil and perfume make the heart glad, So a man's counsel is sweet to his friend." Proverbs 27:9

Preface

In 1975, my wife, Kay, and I visited Reichardt and Elizabeth Taylor, in Uruaçu, Brazil. I was overseeing five churches in the area at the time. Conversation turned to my concern about the lack of enthusiasm and spiritual hunger of so many long-time Christians. I also shared frustration concerning how to encourage on-going vital faith in the church.

In response, Reichardt said, "Maybe this will help," and gave me a set of cassette tapes by Malcolm Smith. I wondered how a series on the blood covenant could minister to me.

I took the tapes with me on a trip to a little church at Morro Agudo (Pointed Hill) in rural Brazil. I arrived a couple of hours early, trudged up the hill, climbed a tree at the top, and settled into the crook of a limb, overlooking the countryside below.

As I listened to the first cassette, my heart erupted in praise, and I nearly fell out of the tree with excitement over new insights I gained into the Last Supper and of once-obscure Bible passages. Perched on that hilltop, I saw more clearly who I am in Christ and the nature of my relationship with Him. My deeper understanding of the ancient ritual of blood covenanting helped me understand what it means to be one with the living God. Through those messages my walk with the Lord was transformed.

Years of studying the ancient rite of blood covenanting, biblical heroes, and covenants in the Bible further confirmed my conviction that all Christians need to understand the ancient ritual and what it means for us today.

After helping me research and listening to me teach hundreds of sessions on the topic, Kay worked with me to compile what we've learned so we can share it with you. Our hope and prayer is that as you read The Great Exchange, the insights gained will impact your faith and transform your lives, as it has ours.

Chapter 1

The Ritual of Blood Covenant

As Jesus and His disciples sat around their final Passover meal together, Jesus took bread, blessed it, broke it, gave it to His disciples, and said, "take, eat, this is My body" (Matt. 26:26). Eat my body? What did Jesus mean when He told His disciples to eat His body?

As if that were not strange enough, He then took a cup of wine, gave thanks, and said, "Drink from it all of you, for this is My blood . . ." (Matt. 26:27–28a). Christians have been called cannibals because of Jesus' invitation to eat His body and drink His blood. Yet, if asked what Jesus was talking about, most Christians could not answer.

Why would He say such a thing to His disciples? Jesus often explained how His teachings applied to life so His listeners would comprehend the message. For example, when telling the parables of the lost sheep and lost coin, Jesus said, "In the same way, I tell you, there is joy in the presence of the angels of God over one sinner who repents" (Luke 15:10). When sharing that the kingdom of heaven is like a dragnet cast into the sea, He finished by saying, "So it will be at the end of the age; the angels shall come forth and take out the wicked from among the righteous . . ." (Matt. 13:49–50).

Many parables end with such application. However, Jesus didn't give an explanation when He shared the story about the man sowing good seed in the field only to have the enemy come behind him and sow tares (weeds) among the wheat. Later, when the disciples were alone with Jesus, they asked, "Explain to us the parable of the tares of the field" (Matt. 13:36).

The disciples were not afraid to ask questions. Rather, they sought understanding. So, why didn't they ask for clarification when He told them to eat His body and drink His blood? After all, to us, those are among the most mysterious words that He said.

Many disciples found his message difficult. However, they didn't question his meaning because they understood the significance of eating His flesh and drinking His blood. They knew exactly what Jesus intended. No further explanation was needed.

Jesus was asking His disciples to join with Him in a blood covenant. The ancient rite of cutting a blood covenant was familiar in their society. They knew the ritual and understood the significance of eating flesh and drinking blood as part of a covenant ritual.

As followers of Jesus today, we need to know what it means to eat His body and drink His blood, and to understand the symbolism in our actions as we celebrate the Lord's Supper. Furthermore, we need to be familiar with the ancient blood covenant ritual behind the ceremony in order to understand the nature of the relationship we have with our Lord.

What Is a Blood Covenant?

A blood covenant is the most binding of agreements. In the East, covenant relationships are even closer and more binding than family ties. Indeed, a friend by covenant is closer than a brother by birth. In the West, we say, "Blood is thicker than water," but the Arabs have a different saying. They say, "blood is thicker than milk." Two children nourished at the same breast are called "milk-brothers,"[1] therefore, people joined by blood covenant are closer than two brothers born from the same parents. In some cultures, a marriage between those whose parents were linked by a blood covenant was deemed incestuous.[2]

Although the concept of covenant is almost unknown in the Western world today, during biblical times, the people "lived in the atmosphere of covenants as in the air they breathed."[3] To people all over the world, it was common practice, and was understood by everyone.[4] Even in recent history, it was common in many places, including Africa, the Middle East, and among Native Americans. However, as time passed, crucial elements were omitted or changed, leaving only semblances of the ancient ritual.

In history, literature, and in scripture there are many records of making covenants. Covenant "supplies the framework for understanding all parts of the Old and New Testaments."[5] In the Greek, a single word is translated either as "covenant" or "testament." The very names *Old Testament/Covenant* and *New Testament/Covenant* tell us that covenant is the central theme of God's Word to us, and yet many of God's people have been oblivious to the significance of the covenant for centuries.

Covenant speaks of relationship, and a blood covenant forms the closest relationship possible. It is significant that God chose to join with Abram in a blood covenant. It is also meaningful to see the circumstances in which it took place.

Rather than covering all the covenants in Scripture, our focus will be on the Abrahamic Covenant, which is the Old Covenant, and on the New Covenant, which is in Jesus Christ.

Abraham Needed a *What?*

In Genesis 15, Abram was old and childless when God promised him he would have a great reward. In those days, an inheritance was useless without children to pass it on to. Consequently, the Lord assured Abram that his heir would come from his own body, and that his descendants would be as numerous as the stars. Because Abram believed God's promise—in spite of his advanced age—he was called righteous.[6]

God then promised to give land to Abram and assured him it would be his. But the land was occupied. How could he take it from those who now possessed it? By that time, Abram had walked over it and seen the fortified cities and the giants there. He was a peaceable man. It was too much for him to imagine that the land on which he was standing would be his. His faith was not big enough to encompass such a promise. It was too much to comprehend.

Abram's response to God was to question Him.[7] Abram said, "How shall I know?" The phrase is also translated, "Whereby shall I know?" The questioning word means *what* (interrogative *what*) or *thing.*[8] Were Abram alive today, we might read that when God spoke to him, he replied, "Say what?"

What Abram asked was, "God, by what can I know that You mean what You just said? God, I need a *what*, a thing, so that I will know." It is significant that Abram asked a "*what*" question.

What is a pronoun. It takes the place of a noun—a thing that is concrete and has substance. When we're not sure we can believe God, we want something with substance. A thing we can touch, feel and see—one that is concrete enough to answer any uncertainty. Something specific that will leave us sure we heard what we think we heard.

That is what Abram was looking for. Something substantive. In two short verses he moved from being a man of faith to a man of uncertainty. He asked God for something concrete, but he left the decision of what to God.

Notice that God did not rebuke Abram for asking. He was neither surprised nor offended by the question. He knew that Abram was having trouble believing, and He wanted to strengthen his faith.

In response to Abram's question, God gave him a *what* by which he could know and believe. He made a blood covenant with him. Through the most sacred of rituals in that society, the doubts were removed from Abram's mind. In fact, God called him the Father of Faith. Because we need the same kind of assurance, we will look at the nature of a blood covenant, at Abram's life, and at others who can teach us what it means to walk in a covenant relationship.

The Nature of a Blood Covenant

When I was a boy I loved to read comic books and go to the movies, especially Westerns. Through them, I learned about Native Americans becoming blood brothers. The mysterious ritual that bonded two people together intrigued me. Seeking the same kind of relationship, a friend and I pricked our fingers and held them together. As we attempted to follow (however poorly) the primitive ritual, we had no idea how ancient it was. Nor did we understand the all-inclusive nature of the commitment made between blood brothers.

Covenants were made for various reasons. Tribal heads often united for protection from a common foe or to strengthen their position through increased land, peoples, or resources. In more recent years, a traveler might join in covenant with a hostile chief in order to insure his safe travels. Henry M. Stanley, who first journeyed to Africa searching for David Livingstone in 1871, made over fifty such covenants in his travels through Africa.[9] Sometimes two men, like Jonathan and David, cut a blood covenant because they had a special affection for or affinity with each other.*

*Later, covenants were made between Lords and vassals, with each pledging loyalty to the other and each gaining from the relationship. These were called suzerainty treaties. They were an adaptation of the blood covenant, but are different from what we are considering because they were made to ensure the loyalty of the vassal to the Lord.

Through the sacred ritual of blood covenanting, men united in purpose, direction, possessions, riches, poverty, and relationship. With so much at stake, blood covenants were normally established only with friends who were trusted and were of a similar status in society.

The rite was so sacred that witnesses would agree to kill their own friend if he was not faithful to fulfill his vow. The covenant makers also called on nature and on God (or gods) to be their witness(es), and they expected dire consequences if they were unfaithful. "The idea that the sky above one's head, the land beneath his feet, and the gods of the territory are all prepared to avenge a violation of the covenant was usually enough to guarantee fidelity of both partners."[10] Thus, the blood covenant became known as an unbreakable covenant.

Marriage is a blood covenant, but is not treated as such because people rarely understand the meaning of the ancient ritual. When Eve was created, God declared, "For this cause a man shall leave his father and his mother, and shall cleave to his wife; and they shall become one flesh" (Gen. 2:24). Becoming one flesh is covenant talk.

Jesus confirmed God's intention that marriage is a blood covenant relationship when He said, "'Have you not read . . . a man shall leave his father and mother, and shall cleave to his wife; and the two shall become one flesh?' Consequently they are no longer two, but one flesh. What therefore God has joined together, let no man separate" (Matt. 19:5–6).

The purpose of this book is to look at how the blood covenant affects our relationship with God, so we will not discuss the wedding ceremony further. However, notes have been added through the remainder of this chapter to document how a present day, Western wedding ceremony compares to a blood covenant.*

*Today, signatures of witness are required on a valid marriage license. However, as witnesses sign their names, they are no longer committing themselves to kill their friends should they be unfaithful to their covenant commitment.

The Seven Exchanges of the Ancient Ritual

Seven key elements were included in the solemn pageant of cutting a blood covenant, and the rite was usually held with ritualistic pomp appropriate for a great occasion. There might be some variation in the order of the ritual, but each step is important because each represents a different pledge, or exchange, of the covenant.

1. Exchange of Cloaks

In the exchange of cloaks, with great ceremony, two men stood before witnesses, removed their cloaks, and traded them with each other. The exchange of cloaks signifies an exchange of their possessions and a promise of provision. In essence, as each presented his cloak to the other, he was saying, "All I am and all I possess, I give to you. Everything I have is now yours. You have access to whatever is mine whenever you want it. This includes my possessions, my status in society, my reputation—anything and everything I have now belongs to you. With my possessions, I will care for you and provide for you whenever you are in need."

Putting on the new cloak represented agreement of the exchange. The two held in common their homes, flocks, bank accounts, servants, and even their families. They were handed over freely, because they belonged to the other. Only the wife was not shared.

In ancient days, the outer garments were made by hand. The quality of the material, the way it was made, how much cloth was used, and the pattern all signified something of the status and occupation of the wearer. Each was distinctive, unique, and personal to the owner, revealing a man's identity long before his face was distinct. For example, Joseph's brothers knew Joseph from afar when they saw his multi-colored cloak.[11]

As men traded cloaks, they also exchanged identity, as the unique robe of each now became the robe of the other. The identity, the resources, and the reputation of the two now became one.*

*A Western wedding ceremony does not include an exchange of cloaks, but traditional marriages do include the concept of shared resources and reputation, where the two become one.

2. Exchange of Weapons

Next, wearing their new cloaks, the two men faced each other and exchanged weapons. They traded bow and arrows, sword, and shield, signifying a promise of giving their strength and protection to the other. With the exchange of weapons they conveyed, "I will give my life to protect you. Your enemies are now my enemies. Your battles are now mine. If you go to war, I will go with you. If anyone comes against you, I will be there for your defense. If anyone attacks you, I will hunt him down and get revenge—even if it costs my life."

The men in the exchange gave their best as a symbol of giving their all in the defense of each other. Only their best would do as they proclaimed protection to one another. In offense and in defense, the two would now be as one.*

*A marriage ceremony does not include an exchange of weapons, but it is generally assumed that the husband, as the stronger, will be the protector of his wife and family. A wife is committed to protecting her husband's reputation.

3. Exchange of Names

Two men making a covenant also exchanged a portion of their names. If Nathan Wilson made a covenant with Joshua Stewart, he added the name *Joshua* or *Stewart* to his own name. He then became known as Nathan Joshua Wilson, Nathan Wilson Stewart, or Nathan Joshua Stewart. Joshua Stewart would take part of Nathan Wilson's name into his in the same manner.

The two became known as one, with one more aspect of their identity shared. Whenever one introduced himself, he would also be introducing his blood brother. If one made a commitment or signed his name on a document, the other was included. If one made a pledge to something, he would be pledging his blood brother as well. Each shared with the other in all obligations, liabilities, and advantages of the name.*

*In most cultures there continues to be some kind of sharing of names after marriage. In many, the woman takes part of the man's name. In others, the man also takes on part of the woman's name. Even if names are not exchanged, it is common for obligations, liabilities, and advantages of the union to be shared by both.

4. Exchange of Blood

The greatest distinctive of the blood covenant, and the source of its name, was the ritual of cutting the flesh. Without bloodletting, it would not be a blood covenant. Generally, the head of the family or tribe was the one who cut the covenant, so it was usually between men, but the rest of the household or tribe were included as part of the pact. They usually cut themselves in a very visible place on the body, such as on the chest, forehead, or wrist. The most common place was to cut the wrist or arm.

If they cut the wrist, the two clasped hands, or brought their wrists together. As the blood flowed from each, it co-mingled and ran down as one. It was then no longer two streams of blood, but one stream. If the cut was elsewhere on the body, the two rubbed the cuts together or joined in some way so the blood co-mingled. In some cultures, something was rubbed into the cut to make the scar more visible. The scar became a reminder of the covenant relationship and a protection from strangers.

We understand that life is in the blood. When God told Noah to sacrifice animals after the flood, He told him not to eat the blood of the animals because the life is in the blood.[12] However, in ancient times, the belief was held that the blood *is* the life of the human being, "not merely that the blood is *essential* to life, but that in a peculiar sense, it *is* life."[13] The perception was that, as blood from the two men flowed together, their lives literally flowed together and became one life. As the blood co-mingled, the men were no longer two, but one.

Of all covenants, only the blood covenant represents joined lives rather than common commitments or agreements. The co-mingling of the blood, and thus the joining of the two lives into one, makes the blood covenant stronger than any other covenant that can be made. The two become one person with two expressions.*

*While the wedding ceremony does not include the co-mingling of blood, the consummation of marriage does involve co-mingling of life as the hymen is torn and blood mixes with semen—both representative of life. Therefore, the lives of two are joined into one. In ancient Hebrew weddings, the couple would retire to a tent and seal the union during the wedding feast. (See Genesis 29:21–23.)

Traditional greetings of a culture offer clues to the importance of covenanting in that culture. Interestingly, in the Far East and the Middle East, which have strong traditions of blood covenanting, the common greeting is a bow or nod. Historically, the only people who shook hands were blood brothers. It is likely that the handshake evolved from the ritual of grasping hands for the blood to flow together. If that is the case, the symbolism of the handshake has become meaningless in Western society, and increasingly so around the world.

In some cultures, people greet by raising their hands. I became familiar with this through seeing Native Americans raise their hands in greetings in movies, but I didn't understand the significance of the gesture. When greeting a stranger with a raised hand, it would be obvious if there were a scar on the wrist. Seeing a scar, the stranger was warned that a blood brother was around somewhere. Because he didn't know who the blood brother was or how big and powerful he was, he would be cautious in his dealings—lest he should cause offense and a blood brother should come looking for him.

If it were an important blood covenant affecting many people, like a covenant between two kings or two warlords, they might also cut an animal in the ritual of bloodletting. They demonstrated the importance of a particularly important covenant by spilling more blood, thus symbolizing more life being given. They split the animal in two from head to tail and laid the pieces opposite one another, with blood likely covering them and the ground. The two then walked between the animal pieces, symbolically saying, "May it be done to me as it has been to this animal, should I not be faithful to keep the commitment I am making this day."

Through the cutting of the flesh, the commitment moved beyond a joining of possessions, protection, and identity. As the blood co-mingled, the two were co-mingled, joined by their very lives. It was not seen as symbolic, but as a literal joining of lives.

There are stories of Norsemen lifting the sod and lying under it as their blood flowed together. Through this, they symbolized their death to their individual, separate lives, and the intermingling of those lives as they lay in their temporary grave. They would then rise "again with a common life—one life, one soul, in two bodies."[14]

5. Exchange of Blessings and Curses

Usually as part of the ceremony of cutting the flesh, the parties entering into covenant proclaimed blessings and curses to one another. They stated the terms of the covenant, such as: "All that I am and all that I have is now yours: all of my camels, all of my sheep, all of my silver and gold. All of my lands and my servants, my sons and my daughters—all are available to you should you ever need them."

If animals were cut as a part of the ceremony, blessings and curses were spoken as part of the bloodletting ceremony. Once the animal was split in two from head to tail, the two men walked among the pieces in a figure eight. As they walked, they moved in blood—in life—and they spoke words of life to one another.*

*A figure eight is made of two circles, which come together without a beginning or an end. In a sense, they are one circle. The two are one, joined, with no beginning or end—throughout eternity, thus depicting the unbreakable nature of the covenant. Interestingly, in math the joined circles on its side are the symbol for infinity.

Numerous and lavish blessings were spoken, to be fulfilled if the covenant was honored and kept. For example, "May your lands be fruitful, and your wives have many children. May they all be healthy and prosperous. May you have an abundance of cattle. . . . As you keep this covenant, may all these blessings come to you."

After the blessings, they stopped, stood on opposite ends of the animals, pointed their finger at each other, and pronounced horrible curses. Their words conveyed, "If you ever break the terms of this covenant, may you be as this animal, split in two, with your blood soaking the ground. May all of your sheep throw their lambs. May all of your crops wilt and die. May all of your herds be stolen. May your wives be ravaged and your children be killed." They continued with a strong, angry tone of voice, pronouncing numerous terrible curses on the other should they ever break the covenant.**

**Declaration of curses is not part of the Western wedding ceremony. (Maybe the divorce rate would decrease if it were!) However, words spoken during the toast at the wedding feast are reminiscent of speaking blessings and likely evolved from the ancient ritual.

6. Memorial Exchange

The making of such a total commitment to one another affected many people besides themselves. It would shape their households—servants as well as family—for generations to come. Their neighbors, and any who did business with them—or had a disagreement with them—could also be greatly affected. Any event with such far-ranging implications needed a reminder of the occasion.

Therefore, a memorial to commemorate the covenant was sometimes given as a gift. They often raised a large stone, possibly with an appropriate inscription scratched on its surface. Sometimes, seven stones were selected to represent the seven exchanges of the covenant; sometimes blood was dripped on them. The memorial served as a reminder to future generations.*

*Today, rings are shared during a wedding ceremony and are a constant memorial of the man and woman being joined as one. The ring serves as a reminder to the wearer as well as an announcement to newcomers that the wearer has been joined with another. Sometimes an inscription is carved inside the ring.

They also might plant a tree at an oasis. As people went to the oasis to draw water, the story would be repeated that it was a covenant tree. Through the retelling, the children, grandchildren, and all who passed by were reminded of the pact.

The Bible mentions several memorials between friends. For example, Abraham gave Abimelech, king of Gerar,** seven ewes as a memorial gift and he planted a grove.[15] Those sheep would be set aside and tended separately from other flocks. It was called a covenant herd, and was given favorable treatment. The special care would invite the telling of its significance. The memorial could be a variety of things, but was always something visible, tangible, and permanent.

**Abimelech is the second ruler that took Sarah into his harem after Abraham declared her as his sister (Gen. 20). Later Abimelech saw that God was blessing Abraham and he approached Abraham seeking covenant (Gen. 21:22ff). After agreeing to a covenant, Abraham complained because Abimelech's servants had been stealing water from Abraham's sheep and oxen.

Whatever the gift, it served as a testimony to generations to come. Once a covenant was cut, it continued throughout the generations, to the children yet unborn, so the monument needed to last through the generations. For as long as it was honored, it was an everlasting covenant, for once two become one, they can't be taken apart.

7. Covenant Meal

Finally, there was a covenant meal. It could be a great feast or a simple ceremony. During the joyous but solemn celebration, words of covenant were spoken to one another. Those who partook of the celebration meal were witnesses to the covenant. Being a witness implied agreement and responsibility to help uphold the terms of the covenant the two covenanters were making with each other.

During the covenant meal, the two men rose and came together with much solemnity. They each took from a loaf of bread and said to the other, "Take, and eat. This represents my body. As you eat this, you are taking my body into yourself."

Then they took a glass of grape juice or wine. They offered the glass to each other saying, "Take this and drink it. This represents my life-blood. As you drink this, you are taking me into yourself."*

*The wedding reception is a clear carry-over from the covenant meal. When the bride and groom feed each other cake and punch, it mimics the ritual exchange of ingesting the body and blood of the other, and thus becoming one indeed.

Through the cutting of flesh, their blood had co-mingled, but with the meal, they went a step further. By eating the bread and drinking the wine, they symbolically took the flesh and blood of the other into themselves, thus becoming one in flesh and in blood. They were co-mingled in such a way that it was impossible to separate them. Thus, the blood covenant was established, and the two indeed were one.**

**Some ancient cultures actually drank blood mixed with the wine. However, drinking of blood was forbidden by God, so was not practiced by the Hebrew people, or apparently by most cultures. It is a perversion of a godly blood covenant. Interestingly, grape juice is sometimes called, "the blood of the grape," thus confirming its symbolic substitution for the blood (Gen. 49:11, Deut. 32:14).

Covenant is "probably the least understood, yet most important concept in the entire Bible . . . It is at once the heart and the foundation of mankind's relationship with God."[16] By understanding the ritual of blood covenanting, we can understand the nature of the relationship God wants with us.

God took the initiative to make that relationship clear. It was through covenant that Abraham gained a foundation for his faith that could withstand testing. As we understand our covenant relationship with God, our faith will also grow. In order to increase our understanding, we will look more closely at the biblical record of covenanting, beginning with Abraham.

The Blood Covenant Ritual

Ritual	Symbolism/Interpretation
Exchange of Cloak	Promise of provision/possessions Exchange of identity
Exchange of Weapons	Promise of protection
Exchange of Names	Identities joined Responsibilities shared
Exchange of Blood	Joining of two lives into one Mark of covenant
Blessings and Curses	Speak blessings for faithfulness Speak curses for unfaithfulness
Exchange of Memorial Gifts	Permanent reminder of the covenant
Exchange of Bread and Wine	Taking in flesh and blood of one another Two are joined as one Celebration of Covenant

Chapter 1 Questions for Reflection and Discussion

1. What picture of blood covenants have you had from history or from childhood stories?

2. How has your understanding of the blood covenant ritual and its symbolism changed?

3. What has the Lord done in your life to give you something concrete—a *what*—to confirm His faithfulness and His desire to be part of your life?

4. How does this add to your understanding of:
   a. marriage?
   b. the Lord's Supper?

5. Read John 17:8–12. The Bible is divided into the Old Testament/Covenant and the New Testament/Covenant. In light of what you have learned about the ancient ritual of cutting a blood covenant, what do these verses say to you?

Chapter 2

God Cuts a Covenant

Abram needed something with substance, a *what,* to help him believe God's promise of the land. God's response to Abram not only had substance, which formed the foundation of Abram's faith, it also defined the relationship God desired with Abram—and with all who follow him. God cut a covenant with Abram, establishing the most intimate relationship possible. Only through a relationship with the living God could Abram learn that He was faithful and could be trusted.

The Covenant Between God and Man

If we look at the scriptural record of the life of Abram, we can confirm the steps of the ancient ritual. The covenant God cut with Abram is a vivid scriptural record of covenant making.

We get our first insight into their relationship in Genesis 12:1 when God spoke directly to Abram, telling him to leave Haran and continue to the land God would show him. God appeared to Abram again in Genesis 15:1 saying, "After these things, the *word* of the LORD came unto Abram *in a vision, saying*" (KJV, emphasis added). The Hebrew for *word* is *dabar*, which also means *matter*, or *thing*. God didn't just talk to him. Like matter, the word that came to Abram had substance. It was based on pictures, action and deep symbolism. God did not just *say* something to Abram; He came to him in word *and* in vision. More precisely, the word itself was in a vision.

Abram experienced something—something with substance as God cut a blood covenant with him. Generally, a vision uses more of the senses and stirs more emotion. Could it be that the word of God came to Abram in a vision because the Lord wanted to be sure that he heard the message and that he never forgot it? This was important to God and He ensured that Abram heard the word.

1. Exchange of Weapons

"The word of the Lord came to Abram in a vision, saying, 'Do not fear, Abram, I am a shield to you'" (Gen. 15:1a). God is saying to Abram, "*I* am your shield and protection. I am your defense." God does not have swords, shields, and armor to exchange in making a blood covenant. He gave Himself instead.

When God told Abram, "I am your protection!" He prefaced His promise with the words, "Do not fear." With God as his shield, would Abram have anything to fear? God's word to him was a covenant commitment.

God doesn't ask anything of Abram at this point—or need anything. If Abram had the best weapons in the world, would God need those for His protection? No. Abram has nothing to give. It is a one-sided exchange because the almighty God does not need or want Abram's help in His defense.

2. Exchange of Cloaks

God follows the proclamation of protection with, "I am thy exceeding great reward" (Gen. 15:1b KJV). God did not have a cloak to give Abram. If God had given a cloak, symbolizing giving of all He had, no man nor people could contain it all. It is impossible; He made the heavens and the earth. Therefore, God is saying to Abram, "Out of the vastness of who I am, I will reward you."

If God rewarded Abram, he would be blessed. If He gave him a great reward, his cup would run over. However, God didn't stop there. He said, "I am thy *exceeding great* reward," ensuring Abram of provisions more abundant than he would ever need.

The reward Abram would receive from God is even broader than physical provision. In the declaration, "I am thy reward," God gave Himself. No gift is more precious than the giving of self. And no gift is greater than God giving of Himself.

Because a covenant is an exchange, it would be understood that Abram would also give of himself and all he had to God. Later, Abram was tested by the Lord to see if he gave his all to God.

Abram was in his eighties and Sarai in her seventies when God first told Abram that He would give the land to his descendents.[1] Even as impossible and ridiculous as descendants seemed at his age, he did not ask for clarification.

However, later (Gen. 15:1) when God spoke to Abram of being his shield and his reward, Abram had questions. Could it be He questioned because He heard God talking covenant talk? His reply to God suggests that was the case.

In response to God's declarations, Abram asks, "O Sovereign LORD, what can you give me since I remain childless and the one who will inherit my estate is Eliezer of Damascus?" . . . "You have given me no children; so a servant in my household will be my heir?" (Gen. 15:2–3 NIV). He is saying, "God, why would you make covenant with me and give me an exceeding great reward? I don't even have a son to pass it down to. I only have a servant that would inherit everything."

Abram's prompt statement, "But, God, I don't have an heir!" is an indication that he understands God is speaking to him in covenant terms. When men cut a covenant, they become the head of a covenant that passes through the generations. Abram is saying, "What is the use of You being all this to me and bringing me into this kind of relationship, if it is only for me?"

Many would be thrilled to have such a promise for their own consumption, with no thought of generations to come. However, Abram, and the culture of his day, understood blood covenants and had vision for the future. He questioned, "If I don't have anybody to pass it on to, what's the use?"

God responded with a promise, "Then the word [*dabar* = matter, thing] of the LORD came to him." God told Abram that Eliezar, his steward, would not be his heir, but a son from his own body would be. He then took Abram outside and said, "Look up at the heavens and count the stars—if indeed you can count them." Then He said to him, "So shall your offspring be." Abram believed the Lord, and He credited it to him as righteousness (Gen. 15:4–6 NIV). Abram believed what God was saying in spite of the evident physical impossibilities. Believing brought him into right relationship with God.

Earlier when the Lord said He would give the land to Abram and his descendents (Gen. 12:7), Abram didn't question God. However, now, when God told Abram He was going to give him the land, Abram's faith was stretched. God said, "I am the LORD who brought you out of Ur of the Chaldeans, to give you this land to possess it." Abraham responded, "O LORD God, how may I know that I shall possess it?" (Gen. 15:7–8). The Hebrew word for "how" is an interrogative that can be translated, "how?" "what?" or "anything."[2]

As we discussed in the previous chapter, Abram is asking, "God, how will I know what You are saying is true? By *what* will I know that I will inherit it? Give me something of substance." After seeing the giants and strongholds throughout Canaan, he didn't have faith to believe God could give him the land. Abram needed a thing, a *what.* God told him to go get some animals. He made the covenant to give Abram a *what.* God didn't need to make the covenant. His Word was good without a guarantee. Still, God met Abram in his need for something substantive to help him believe.

3. a. Bloodletting: Cutting the Animals

In response to Abram's question, "By what shall I know?" God told Abram to "Take me a heifer of three years old, and a she goat of three years old, and a ram of three years old, and a turtledove, and a young pigeon." Abram brought them all and "divided them in the midst, and laid each piece one against another [opposite each other], but the birds he divided not" (Gen. 15:9–10 KJV).

The animals are clearly being cut for the purpose of a blood covenant ritual. There is no other reason to divide animals down the middle and then lay them opposite each other. For burnt offerings, the animals were cut differently and were not laid out on the ground.

As the sun was setting, Abram fell into a deep sleep, "and behold, terror and great darkness fell upon him" (Gen. 15:12). After the sun set it was very dark, "and behold, there appeared a smoking oven and a flaming torch which passed between these pieces. On that day the LORD made a covenant with Abram, saying, 'To your descendants I have given this land.'" (Gen. 15:17–18a).

We can see that this is not just any covenant, but a very important one, because animals were slain for the spilling of more blood. However, not just one animal, but three animals were split down the middle. I believe God told Abram to slay three animals for two reasons: (1) Three animals clearly symbolize the three-fold nature of God, representing the Father, the

Son, and the Holy Spirit. The animals were also three years old, further indicating the trinity. Through the use of the threes, we can see that *all* of God was involved in the covenant. (2) Three animals also spill three times as much blood, representing three times as much life being exchanged. This was not just any covenant—it was a covenant between the almighty God and human kind.

Let's look more closely at the action. Abram laid the animals out opposite each other. Blood was all over the ground. The site was readied for the covenant ritual. The scriptures say God cut this covenant with Abram, but where was Abram during the ceremony?

God caused him to be in a deep sleep—a deep trance. God removed Abram from participating in the rite, allowing him only to watch. If he was asleep during the covenanting ritual, he obviously didn't have anything to do with cutting the covenant. If the covenant was between God and Abram, why didn't Abram take part in the ceremony?

How could the Creator become one with a being that was created by Him? How could a holy, omnipotent, almighty God become one with a fallen man? It is impossible. So God sent a representative for Himself and one for Abram for the ceremony. Abram was only an observer, a witness.

The ritual began after the sun went down when God sent a smoking furnace (oven) and a burning lamp (flaming torch) to pass between the slain animals.[3] Abram's people were a nomadic people. Their ovens were portable clay pots, which they could carry with them when they moved. The coals were placed in the bottom of the clay pot for heat. Abram observed smoke coming out of the top of the oven as it moved in a figure eight among the pieces.

The Holy Spirit has always been God's representative to man. From early church history, smoke has symbolized the Holy Spirit. Abram saw the Spirit representing the Father in the ritual of cutting covenant.*

*When tribal leaders entered into covenant, it was not unusual for a substitute to stand in as representative for the chief.

Abram also saw a flaming torch moving in a figure eight among the pieces. The purpose for a flaming torch is to provide light. Who is the Light of the world? Jesus Christ. Jesus has always been mankind's representative in our relationship with the Father. Therefore, in this most important part of the covenant ritual, as Abram slept, the torch, representing Jesus, stood in for Him in cutting the covenant with the living God. Abram didn't participate.

A holy God could not become one with sinful man, lest He become defiled. It could not be. Light cannot walk with darkness.[4] God took the initiative to meet man in his need by providing a substitute to bridge the gap.

History has shown that man has never been faithful in keeping the covenant. If either party broke the pact, it would be over, and the covenant breaker would be killed. God knew the sinful, self-centered, frail nature of mankind. Because man could not keep the covenant, God used a substitute so the continuing of the covenant would not be dependent on fallen man. Because Jesus stood in for Abram, He guaranteed an eternal, unbroken bond. God could swear by nothing greater, so He swore by Himself. He took one hundred percent of the responsibility.

The very next verse confirms again that it is a blood covenant, "In the same day, the LORD made [Hebrew: *karath*, meaning to cut]** a covenant with Abram" (Gen. 15:18 KJV). God desired to walk in intimate relationship with Abram, and through Jesus Christ, He provided a way to make it possible. "I am come that they might have life, and that they might have it more abundantly" (John 10:10b KJV).

The Hebrew word for "made" is ***karath* (Strongs #H3772), meaning "to cut." In the Bible, it is usually translated as "made." However, sometimes when "made" is used in covenant context, the original Hebrew means "to establish." Consequently, when "made" is ***karath***, or "to cut," we will often make note of it.

God has always provided a way. He *has* called us to faithfulness. It is required of a servant that he be found faithful,[5] but He is not hindered by our weakness. Nor does our sin and weakness cause the covenant to be broken, because God sent a substitute for us. In essence, He cut a covenant with Himself on our behalf.

If the covenant depended on Abram, it would be broken in the first generation. However, because Jesus (our substitute) lived a perfect, sinless life, the covenant could be passed on to a thousand generations—because He will not break it. Because of Jesus, Abraham and his children are secure in their covenant relationship with God.

As we have mentioned, in preparation for cutting the covenant, God told Abram to bring him a heifer, a goat, a ram, a turtledove, and a young pigeon. Abram brought them to God, cut the large animals in two, and laid the halves opposite each other. However, *"he did not cut the birds"* (Gen. 15:9–10, emphasis added).

Although the reason for the two birds that God told Abram to bring is not specified, they must be significant because it is recorded for us to read thousands of years later. God told Abram to bring a turtledove and a young pigeon, but the only further mention of the birds is to say that they were not divided. So, what part did they play in the covenant ritual?

Other times the turtle dove and pigeon are mentioned in scripture, it usually concerned sacrifices for burnt offerings. God makes provision for the poor who cannot afford to sacrifice a larger animal. They may bring a turtledove or pigeon instead.

In Leviticus, the Lord declared that a guilty person can bring an offering of a lamb or goat as a guilt offering for his sin. "*But if he can't afford a lamb, then he shall bring to the LORD . . . two turtledoves or two young pigeons*" (Lev. 5:5–7, emphasis added).

Likewise, after childbirth, a sacrifice was required for purification. The new mother could bring the priest a lamb for a burnt offering to be cleansed from the flow of blood and a turtledove or pigeon for a sin offering. However, "*if she cannot afford a lamb, then she shall take two turtledoves or two young pigeons,* the one for a burnt offering and the other for a sin offering; and the priest shall make atonement for her" (Lev. 12:6–8, emphasis added).

The birds were provision for the poor people as substitutes for the larger animals.[6] The purpose for the sacrifices in which the birds were used was for atonement and cleansing[7] on the people's behalf, so that they would be acceptable before the Lord.[8]

Unlike these accounts of sacrifice, there is no record that Abram sacrificed the birds that God told him to bring. They were there, but they were not divided and did not seem to be a part of the covenant making ritual.

It seems the birds were representatives for Abram and Sarai. Even as God was fully represented, Abram and Sarai were represented. As mankind had nothing to contribute in the making of the covenant, the birds had nothing to contribute. They are smaller, weaker, and poorer—of little or no use. Even as sacrifices, they were a poor man's substitute.

If their blood were spilt in the cutting of the covenant, it would be insignificant in the midst of the blood of the heifer, goat, and ram. Not only would it be of no consequence, it would be out of place, because Abram was not part of the cutting of the covenant—God did it all. Abram had nothing to offer. If God did not provide a way, it would be impossible for the created to join as one with the Creator.

The uncut turtledove and pigeon are a vivid picture of the nature of our covenant with God—we have nothing to offer. We are of no consequence, no significance—except that the Almighty God chose to include us as one with Himself.

3. b. Bloodletting: Cutting the Flesh

God records for us the mark in the flesh in the cutting of the covenant with Abram in Genesis 17:9–13. The blood flowed from Abram and his sons. First, God admonished Abraham, his seed, and their generations to keep the covenant made between Him and them. Then He said:

> Every man child among you shall be circumcised. And ye shall circumcise the flesh of your foreskin: and it shall be a token of the covenant between me and you. And he that is eight days old shall be circumcised. . . . He that is born in thy house, and he that is bought with thy money, must needs be circumcised: and my covenant shall be in your flesh for an everlasting covenant. And the uncircumcised man child whose flesh of his foreskin is not circumcised, that should shall be cut off (*karath*) from his people: he hath broken my covenant. (Gen. 17:10–13 KJV, emphasis added)

Through circumcision, the perpetual and inclusive nature of the covenant is emphasized, as all the male members of the household were to be circumcised along with Abram. Included were the slaves and any foreigner that would join with them as part of the household, and any children (or grandchildren) that were to be born later. It also emphasized the exclusive nature of the covenant in that not just anyone was part of this special relationship with God. If a parent chose not to circumcise his son, he would be breaking the covenant and would be cut off [*karath*]* by God, and was to be cut off by the people of God. The circumcision was the defining sign of covenant membership.

*This is the same Hebrew word that is used for "cut" or "made" a covenant.

As in all blood covenants, God required the cutting of Abram's flesh. However, this mark in the flesh is different than most blood covenants; it is not in a visible place. It was in such a place that it would never be exposed to other people. Abram would know that he was circumcised, but the stranger he met along the way would not know to be cautious with Abram because he had a blood brother who was committed to protecting him.

Instead, Abram would have to call on the name of the Lord, and depend on the Lord to be his shield and protection.

Because people would not see the mark on the wrist, to walk in this blood covenant required faith to trust God to be a shield whenever danger or adversity threatened. God cut a blood covenant to build faith in Abram and his children, but even from the very beginning He required them to operate by faith rather than by sight. God has never wanted His people to function by what they see, but by faith. Faith is the substance of things not seen.[9] The need for faith is a common theme in the Word. "The just (righteous one) shall live by faith" (Heb. 10:38 KJV).

There is another significant difference between the cutting of the flesh in this covenant and other blood covenants. Rather than cutting to let blood flow and leave a mark, flesh is actually removed from Abram. The removal of the flesh is symbolic of what must happen when joining into covenant with the holy God. As sinful men, in order to be one with God, believers must put off flesh.

It is our spirit that joins with God. During the time of Moses, God tells His people not to just circumcise the foreskin, but to circumcise the foreskin of their hearts.[10] When we are in covenant with God, we are to put off our old nature, leaving the things of the flesh behind us.[11]

4. Exchange of Blessings and Curses

There is not a clear record in Scripture of speaking the blessings and the curses between God and Abram in traditional covenant language, but the Lord spoke blessings on several occasions. We have already mentioned the promises to bless Abram with a son and with descendents as numerous as the stars. His promise of land[12] is also a clear blessing.

God also spoke blessings to Abram in Genesis 12:3, "I will bless them that bless thee, and curse him that curseth thee: and *in thee shall all families of the earth be blessed*" (KJV, emphasis added). It is a specific blessing given to Abram, and is applicable to all who are his descendents in covenant.

Historically, the Hebrew people have rested in the knowledge that they were the chosen people of God. However, within the blessing, there is also a mission, as God declared that all the families of the earth were to be blessed through them. It seems that they never caught the vision of God's mission for them.

The blessings continue as God told Abram in Genesis 17, "I will make you "a father of a multitude of nations, . . . exceedingly fruitful, . . . and kings shall come forth from you. And I will establish My covenant between Me and you and your seed after you throughout their generations for an everlasting covenant" (Gen. 17:4, 6–7).

As God reiterates the blessings, He adds, "*I will be their God*" (Gen. 17:7–8). From here on, throughout the Old Testament, God frequently says, "I am your God, you are My people." This is a possessive statement, and is spoken only to those in covenant relationship with Him. There is no greater blessing than having the one true God choose you and declare, "I am your God; you are My people."

The fact that God did not list curses in the cutting of the covenant with Abraham could be indicative of the fact that God wanted a relationship with mankind that was built on love and trust rather than on fear of consequences. While God asks for external compliance with the commandments, He consistently says that it is the heart He is most concerned about. God gave His people hundreds of years to learn to walk in covenant from the heart before he gave them guidelines (laws) to rule their actions.

5. The Memorial

The blessing of a son and the descendants that followed were memorials to the covenant as well as a blessing. Isaac was a visible sign that God was fulfilling His covenant. There was no human way possible for Sarai and Abram to have children at their age. Sarai was biologically beyond the age of childbearing. When God gave them Isaac, it became a testimony and tangible reminder to all around them of their powerful God. The testimony continued and increased as the descendants of Abram became as numerous as the stars.

The land was also a memorial that has remained Isaac's descendants' through the centuries in spite of fierce opposition. God told Abram repeatedly that He would give him the land. It was part of the covenant promise. A major reason Israel is so determined to hold onto the land is the deep conviction it was given to them by God through their father Abraham.

6. The Memorial Meal

A memorial meal is not clearly recorded in scripture for the Abrahamic covenant. However, in Genesis 14:18–20, after Abram defeated the kings who had captured Sodom and Gomorrah, Abram broke bread and drank wine with Melchizedek.

> And Melchizedek king of Salem brought out bread and wine; now he was a priest of God Most High. And he blessed him and said, "Blessed be Abram of God Most High, Possessor of heaven and earth; And blessed be God Most High, Who has delivered your enemies into your hand." And he gave him a tenth of all. (Gen. 14:18–20)

Melchizedek was clearly a representative of God, the elements of the meal were shared, a blessing was spoken (to Abram and to God), and Abram gave him a tithe (maybe as a symbolic representation that all he had was God's). Many elements of a covenant celebration are included. Is it significant that this is just a few verses before God came to Abram in a vision declaring that He was his shield and great reward? The two passages are also linked by the phrase, "After these things." This seems to be the covenant meal, held at the beginning of the ritual, rather than at the end, but it is not clearly defined as one.

In another incident, in Genesis 18, the angels appeared and had a meal with Abraham before going to Sodom and Gomorrah. Even though Abraham said at that point he saw the Lord, and they shared a meal, the meal was not clearly connected to the ritual of covenant making, so I cannot justify saying that the purpose of the meal was to celebrate the covenant.

Since scripture never clearly links "Abram," "covenant." and a "meal" in a single passage, one could be in error to assume anything. Nonetheless it is not a critical issue if the celebration of the meal is not recorded. There is enough other information to substantiate the cutting of a covenant without a record of the meal.

7. Exchange of Names

In Genesis 17, when Abram was ninety-years-old, Scripture shows the completion of the ritual of blood covenanting between God and Abram. First, God confirmed the covenant and called on Abram to walk blameless before Him. In response, Abram fell on his face. Next, God said, "As for Me, behold, My covenant is with you, And you shall be the father of a multitude of nations. *No longer shall your name be called Abram, But your name shall be Abraham*; For I will make you the father of a multitude of nations" (Gen. 17:1–5, emphasis added).

In these verses, God clearly links covenant with the changing of Abram's name to Abraham. However, it is not just a change of names but is an *exchange*. There is a strong, breathy consonant, ה, in YHWH (יהוה), the name of God. It is used twice. God took the most prominent sound **ha** out of His name and added into Abram's. From that day forward, Abram is known as Abraham, with a part of God's name added to his.

It is an awesome thing to think of the holy, living God adding part of His name to a man. However, as God changed Abram's name, He did even more. He also added something of His substance. The letter that was placed in Abram's name was not just any letter. It has a breathy sound that reminds us of the breath of life that God breathed into Adam. This was a significant addition to Abram, as God symbolically added life to his name.Furthermore,

> Then God said to Abraham, "As for Sarai your wife, you shall not call her name Sarai, but Sarah shall be her name. And I will bless her, and indeed I will give you a son by her. Then I will bless her, and she shall be a mother of nations; kings of peoples shall come from her." (Gen. 17:15–16)

From that day on, when her name, Sarah, was spoken, it would also have the breathy sound from the name of God. The inclusion of Sarai in the name change is critical and extremely significant socially and relationally, because God makes it clear that the women are equal with men in relationship with Him. It is not a reflection of exclusivity in the heart of God that men have traditionally been more important in society, or even that it is the man that is usually the covenant maker. In relationship with God, woman is equal with man. Even though God appointed the man as head, and directed the woman to submit, the man is not superior to the woman. He simply holds a different function and responsibility.

The change of names is obvious, but it was also an exchange, for God took on Himself the name of Abraham, expressed by the possessive *of*. From this time forth, He is called the "God *of Abraham*." Later, He was called the God *of Isaac*, and *of Jacob*, and *of Israel*. Through this we can see once again, the generational nature of the covenant. As a covenant was cut with one generation, it continued through their seed to their children and on through the generations. When speaking to Moses, several times God said, "I am the God of your fathers."[13]

He also uses the possessive term, "I am *your* God." The depth of intimacy God desires with His people is significant. We know that we can never truly take possession of God, but He uses the term of Himself so that we will know without a doubt that He has indeed given Himself to us to be *our* God.[14]

Covenant: A Foundation for Faith

When in need of something substantive to help him believe, Abram asked God a simple question, "By what shall I know?" God's response was a word (a message) in a vision—something concrete that would lead to an increase in Abraham's faith.

Abraham now had a foundation for his faith. God had come to him and cut an unbreakable covenant, promising provision, and protection—everything he would ever need. In essence, God, the Almighty God, gave all He is and all He had to Abraham. However, learning to walk in the knowledge and strength of that faith foundation was not without trial and error. Like us, Abraham had to *learn* to walk by faith, and it took time.

Exchanges of the Old Covenant

Ritual and Symbolism/Interpretation	Scriptural Reference
Exchange of Cloak Promise of provision/possessions Exchange of identity	Gen.15:1 I am your reward Gen. 12:1-3 I will bless you Gen. 13:15 Promise of land
Exchange of Weapons Promise of protection	Gen. 15:1 I am a shield to you
Exchange of Names Identities joined Responsibilities shared	Gen. 17:5 Abram to Abraham Gen. 17:15 Sarai to Sarah Gen. 31:42 God of Abraham
Exchange of Blood Cutting human flesh Joining two lives into one Mark of Covenant Cutting of animals Death of self if unfaithful Importance of pact demonstrated	Gen. 17:11 Circumcision Gen. 15:8-18 Heifer, goat, and ram
Exchange of Blessings and Curses Speak Blessings for faithfulness Speak Curses for unfaithfulness	Deut. 28:2-14 Blessings Deut. 28:15-68 Curses
Exchange of Memorial Gifts A permanent witness to and reminder of the covenant	(Not clearly stated in Old Testament) Gen. 12:6-7 The land Gen. 17:19 Isaac (Seven memorials are established with Israel. Chapter 7)
Exchange of Bread (flesh) and Wine (blood) Taking in flesh and blood of one another Two are joined as one Celebration of Covenant	(Not clearly noted in Old Testament) Possibly: Gen. 14:18-20 Abraham and Melchizedek or Gen. 18 Three visitors to Abraham

Chapter 2 Questions for Reflection and Discussion

1. Read Psalms 18:2, 30, 35 and 28:7.
    - What do these passages ask from us in our relationship with God as our shield?
    - Practically and specifically, what does it mean that God is your shield?

2. Read Genesis 15:1 and Psalms 23:1. How does it change *your* life—your faith and actions—to acknowledge that the living God promised Himself to *you* to be your reward?

3. How does it feel to know that your part in the covenant pageant is symbolized by a turtledove and pigeon (Gen. 15:9–10)?

4. When you celebrate the Lord's Supper, what does God want you to remember, other than that Jesus died on the cross for your sins?

5. God has already given all He has and all that He is to those who choose to be one with Him through Jesus Christ. If you belong to Him, it is already yours. What do you need to do to access it?

Chapter 3

Abraham Learns to Walk in Covenant

Abraham had it made. Of all the people on earth, he was chosen by the Most High God, guaranteed full protection, abundant provision, and an intimate relationship with the living, loving, faithful God. In return, the Lord asked only that he be faithful and obedient. It would seem that Abraham was assured success. However, it took him years and major failures before he learned to walk in covenant with the living God.

Although we face the same challenges Abraham did, he had one advantage: he was familiar with the covenant ritual and understood the comprehensive nature of the commitment made in a blood covenant. Abraham also had major disadvantages. He did not have a heritage of knowing God. The written Word was not available to him. He also grew up in a family and a culture that worshipped many gods, so he did not have friends or neighbors to point him to the Lord or answer his questions.

God taught Abraham to walk in covenant in spite of his pagan background. As we look at his life during the training process, three things become evident: 1) throughout the years, God was covenantally faithful, even when Abraham was not faithful in return, 2) Abraham's faith increased as he learned that God is always faithful, and 3) the relationship between God and Abraham was strengthened as Abraham matured in his knowledge of God and of what it means to walk in covenant.

Abram's Early Relationship with God

Even though he did not know God yet, when "the LORD had said to Abram, 'Leave your country, your people and your father's household and go to the land I will show you'" (Gen. 12:1), Abram obeyed God's call—in spite of the lack of an appointed destination. He took his whole household, including his wife, Sarai, his nephew, Lot, and all his possessions (v. 5) and began a nomadic move to an unknown land.

When he arrived in Canaan, the Lord appeared to him and said, "To your descendants I will give this land" (Gen. 12:7). Abram then built an altar to God. After traveling to a mountain between Bethel and Ai, he pitched his tent and built another "altar to the LORD and called upon the name of the LORD" (Gen. 12:8). In this recorded interchange between God and Abram, he acknowledged God and chose to obey Him, to worship Him, and to call on His name.

Cultures that worship many gods are often fearful, lest they displease one of the gods. They perform religious rituals in order to keep the gods happy. Abram came from such a culture. His obedience and worship were probably motivated by fear of displeasing *a* god rather than by love or relationship with the Almighty God.

It is clear that Abram didn't know God's ways at the time he and Sarai fled to Egypt because of a severe famine. While there, he devised a scheme, because he was concerned for his safety. He said to Sarai,

> I know that you are a beautiful woman; and it will come about when the Egyptians see you, that they will say, "This is his wife"; and they will kill me, but they will let you live. Please say that you are my sister so that it may go well with me because of you, and that I may live on account of you." (Gen. 12:11–13)*

*Since Sarai was his half-sister as well as wife, Abram did not totally lie to Pharaoh, but he was deceptive in choosing to hide their marital relationship.

Fear caused Abram to think only of himself. However, before we judge him, we need to realize that Abram's relationship with God was young. Furthermore, he had grown up in a pagan society and a culture where women were considered little more than possessions.

Why should Abram trust God to protect him? He had never witnessed other gods give protection, so he had no reason to expect it of God. In addition, the Lord had not yet cut the covenant with him promising to be his shield. It is no surprise that he looked out for his own well-being.

In spite of Abram's self-centeredness and lack of faith, God intervened on behalf of Sarai and Abram. He dealt covenantally with Abram and Sarai, protecting them even before the covenant was cut. Pharaoh's officials did notice Sarai's beauty and she was taken into Pharaoh's house. In return, Abram received favor from Pharaoh and was given sheep, oxen, donkeys and camels, as well as male and female servants. "But the LORD struck Pharaoh and his house with great plagues because of Sarai, Abram's wife" (Gen. 12:17).

> Then Pharaoh called Abram and said, "What is this you have done to me? Why did you not tell me that she was your wife? Why did you say, 'She is my sister,' so that I took her for my wife? Now then . . . take her and go." And . . . they escorted him away, with his wife and all that belonged to him. (Gen. 12:15–20)

Abram's Dealings with Lot

When Abram returned to Canaan, the land was not rich enough to support the vast number of livestock owned by Abram and his nephew, Lot. Tension over grazing rights arose among the herdsmen.[1] God had promised the whole territory to Abram, and Lot's only claim to the land was that he was part of Abram's extended family. Therefore, Abram had the right to choose whatever land he wanted, giving Lot what was left over. However, he chose to defer to Lot, saying, "Please let there be no strife between you and me, nor between my herdsmen and your herdsmen, for we are brothers. Is not the whole land before you? Please separate from me: if to the left, then I will go to the right; or if to the right, then I will go to the left" (Gen. 13:8–9).

Lot chose the rich valley along the Jordan River where water was plentiful—leaving Abram with the hill country of Canaan. With the fertile ground, Lot inherited life with a society that was "exceedingly wicked and [sinful] against the LORD" (Gen. 13:13). In contrast, with his allotment of mountain land, Abram received an inheritance from God.

Through deferring the choice to Lot, Abram began to experience God as his provision. The Lord rewarded Abram for his faith and lack of selfishness by appearing to him immediately and promising blessings of land and descendants.[2] Through the years, Abram was also blessed with prosperity, even though he had the less fertile land.

Lot eventually settled in the city of Sodom. Later, the citizens of the city, including Lot and all his possessions, were carried away.[3] Abram pursued and attacked in spite of the fact that he was not a warrior. Although the covenant was not yet cut, God empowered and protected Abram, giving him a great victory. Through the battle, Abram learned God would protect and empower him.

However, what is recorded of Abram's attitude toward God is as significant as the victory. As the one who led in the battle, Abram earned a share of the spoil, but he refused it, saying, "I have sworn to the LORD God Most High, possessor of heaven and earth, that I will not take a thread or a sandal thong or anything that is yours, lest you [the king of Sodom] should say, 'I have made Abram rich'" (Gen. 14:22–23).

Abram recognized God as the Most High God—the God above all gods, and he chose to honor Him rather than enjoy the spoils that were rightfully his. He not only acknowledged and trusted the Lord, he was also willing to give testimony to the power of God and to his dependence upon Him. Abram had moved beyond making choices because he was afraid of displeasing a god. He was learning that God is sovereign, faithful, and dependable. He was also willing to be identified as one who trusted in Him.

When Abram obeyed God and left Haran, he was rewarded by God appearing to him in Canaan with promises of blessings. When he deferred the choice of land to Lot, he was also visited by God with a reiteration of promises of land and provision. As Abram chose to honor God rather than accept the spoils of war, the Lord rewarded him by appearing to him.

"*After these things*, the word of the LORD came to Abram in a vision" (Gen. 15:1, emphasis added). After Abram rescued Lot, after the meal with Melchizadek,[4] after he paid his tithe to God,[5] after he chose to honor the Lord rather than be honored with spoils of war . . . After these things in which Abram proved his heart was turned toward God, the Word of the Lord came to him and God initiated the ritual of covenanting.

God did not force covenant on Abram. He first built a relationship with him and gained his trust and loyalty. He waited until Abram grew in his knowledge of God and in his willingness to trust Him, then He revealed what was on His heart by establishig a blood covenant relationship with him. As recorded in Chapter Two, God told Abram to get three animals; then He moved among the pieces as a flaming torch and a smoking oven. God promised to be Abram's provision and protection, to give him land and descendants, and to bless all the nations of the earth through him.

Abram's Big Mistake

God had promised Abram descendants as numerous as the stars and the dust, saying, "one who shall come forth from your own body, he shall be your heir" (Gen. 15:4). However, Abram waited for years, but there was no sign of a son.

When Abram had lived in Canaan for ten years, Sarai said to him, "Now behold, the LORD has prevented me from bearing children. Please go in to my maid; perhaps I shall obtain children through her" (Gen. 16:2). And Abram listened to the voice of Sarai.

He "went in to Hagar, and she conceived; and when she saw that she had conceived, her mistress was despised in her sight" (Gen. 16:2–4).

Sarai and Abram may have reasoned, "God said an heir would come from *Abram's* bowels, not from Sarai's." Having an heir was important in the culture as well as to fulfill what God had spoken to Abram. Because Sarai had not had a son and was beyond the age of childbearing, they were doing what was reasonable and acceptable in their culture. They did what was reasonable—but reason is not faith. Faith may or may not seem reasonable. Regardless, it is a gift from God that surpasses our mental understanding.

Abram's reasoning failed on several counts: He failed to realize that upon marriage, he became one with Sarai. Therefore, Sarai would be one with him in the expectation that an heir would come from her bowels as well as from his. His lack of experience in knowing God made it impossible for him to take into account the extent God would go to in order to show Himself strong on his behalf. Even though his decision seemed reasonable, he could not see into the future. His lack of faith would have dire implications for centuries to come.*

*Much of the Middle East conflict today is between the descendants of Isaac and of Ishmael. Islam teaches that the promises of God are through Ishmael, rather than through Isaac.

Abram's lack of trust and his efforts to take care of the problem himself had spiritual consequences too. Unlike the times when Abram trusted and God immediately appeared to him, Abram's actions were followed by distance in his relationship with the Lord. Ishmael was born when Abram was eighty-six years old, and God did not appear to Abram again until he was ninety-nine years old.[6] For thirteen years, Abram did not have a personal encounter with God. Meanwhile, he reared Ishmael, whom he believed to be the promised son.

Covenant Friendship

When God finally appeared once again to Abram, He repeated covenant blessings and completed further steps of the covenant ritual. He changed Abram's and Sarai's names to Abraham and Sarah, and directed the circumcision of all males of Abraham's household.[7]

The Lord also spoke to Abraham concerning Sarah: "And I will bless her, and indeed I will give you a son by her. Then I will bless her, and she shall be a mother of nations; kings of peoples shall come from her" (Gen. 17:16).

Abraham's response to God's announcement gives further insight into his heart, and the relationship between him and God. He did not yet understand how powerful his God was. In response to the Lord's announcement, Abraham:

> fell on his face and laughed, and said in his heart, "Will a child be born to a man one hundred years old? And will Sarah, who is ninety years old, bear a child?"
>
> And Abraham said to God, "Oh that Ishmael might live before Thee!"
>
> But God said, "No, but Sarah your wife shall bear you a son, and you shall call his name Isaac; and I will establish My covenant with him for an everlasting covenant for his descendants after him." (Gen. 17:17–19)

Abraham's deep love and hope for his son Ishmael is evident in his plea for Ishmael to "live before" God. For thirteen years, he had seen his son as the heir to the promises of God. All of his dreams were wrapped up in Ishmael, and they were evidently not easily surrendered. If a son were born to Sarah, that would change everything.

God was not offended by Abraham's request on Ishmael's behalf, and proceeded to answer all of his unspoken questions. The son born to Sarah would be the heir of the covenant cut with God. Ishmael, as a son of Abraham would be blessed abundantly, even to having twelve princes and a great nation come from him. However, the covenant would be continued through Isaac.[8]

> And as for Ishmael, *I have heard you; behold, I will bless him*, and will make him fruitful, and will multiply him exceedingly. He shall become the father of twelve princes, and I will make him a great nation. But My covenant I will establish with Isaac. (Gen. 17:20–21, emphasis added)

The Lord's words, "*I have heard you*; behold, I will bless him," indicate that Ishmael was blessed because of Abraham. God honored the request of His covenant partner. Although it may have been difficult for Ishmael to be passed over as the chosen heir of the covenant, Abraham did not let it hinder his obedience to God.

Abraham was circumcised when he was ninety-nine years old. Ishmael, his thirteen-year-old son, was circumcised the same day. All the men of his household, who were born in the house or bought with money from a foreigner, were circumcised with him.[9]

Later, God sent three messengers to Abraham and he served them food. A messenger then asked, "Where is Sarah your wife?" (Gen. 18:9).

> And [Abraham] said, "Behold, in the tent."
>
> And he said, "I will surely return to you at this time next year; and behold, Sarah your wife shall have a son."
>
> And Sarah was listening at the tent door, which was behind him. Now Abraham and Sarah were old, advanced in age; Sarah was past childbearing. And Sarah laughed to herself, saying, "After I have become old, shall I have pleasure, my Lord being old also?"
>
> And the LORD said to Abraham, "Why did Sarah laugh, saying, 'Shall I indeed bear a child, when I am so old?' Is anything too difficult for the LORD? At the appointed time I will return to you, at this time next year, and Sarah shall have a son."
>
> Sarah denied it however, saying, "I did not laugh"; for she was afraid.
>
> And He said, "No, but you did laugh." (Gen. 18:9–15)

Both Abraham and Sarah responded with doubt and laughter at God's declaration that they would have a son. Therefore, God named their son Isaac, which means laughter or mockery.[10] For the rest of their lives, through Isaac's name they were reminded that God is sovereign and is not limited by their faith or by the laws of nature. If they doubted one of God's promises to them, all they had to do was remember the time they laughed at the impossible, only to see God bring it about.

As the messengers who brought news of Isaac were leaving, Abraham accompanied them along the way. Their conversation gives us a peek into the nature of the relationship between him and his God. When the Lord shared His plan to destroy Sodom and Gomorrah, Abraham was bold enough to appeal, illustrating the give and take of dialogue between friends.

While acknowledging that God is sovereign and the decision was in His hands, Abraham pled for saving the cities if fifty righteous souls could be found. When his wish was granted, he continued to bargain, for forty-five souls, then forty, and thirty, until he was down to ten righteous people. The Lord was not impatient as Abraham entreated Him to save the city (Gen. 18:23–32). He agreed to the request of His covenant partner. Likewise, Abraham left it in God's hands, trusting Him with the outcome.

But Abraham's pleas were in vain. The wicked cities did not hold ten righteous people. "Thus it came about, when God destroyed the cities of the valley, that *God remembered Abraham*, and sent Lot out of the midst of the overthrow, when He overthrew the cities in which Lot lived" (Gen. 19:29, emphasis added).

Lot was not living with Abraham at the time of the circumcision, and we have no record that he was circumcised (which would have confirmed that he was in covenant). However, God was faithful to protect him *and* his household—because God remembered Abraham and the covenant he had with him. Once again, Abraham had a very personal lesson that helped him learn the extent of God's covenant faithfulness.

Abraham's Faith Wavers

Abraham, the Father of Faith, did not always exhibit faith. "Now Abraham journeyed . . . and settled between Kadesh and Shur; then he sojourned in Gerar. And Abraham said of Sarah, his wife, 'She is my sister.' So Abimelech king of Gerar sent and took Sarah" (Gen. 20:1–2).

After so much growth in his knowledge of God and relationship with Him, how could Abraham claim his wife as his sister a second time? The Lord had already rescued him in a similar situation. Since that time, He had cut a covenant with Abraham, promising to be his protection. Abraham had also experienced God's protection several other times.

With a history of seeing God as his shield, why did he not trust his God in Gerar?

Even Abimelech asked Abraham why he would do such a thing. Abraham's response is revealing, "Because I thought, Surely the fear of God is not in this place; and they will slay me for my wife's sake" (Gen. 20:10–11).

While Abraham knew God was strong, he wasn't sure Abimelech feared God. Consequently, he doubted God could—or would—protect him.

He noted, "surely the fear of God is not in this place." Would he be safe in his dealings with someone who did not acknowledge the Lord? If Abimelech couldn't see a mark on his wrist, how would he know he was in covenant with the living God? If Abimelech didn't know, then Abraham would surely be killed unless he took measures to protect himself.* Abraham's reasoning misled him again.

*The story of Abraham and Abimelech continues in Genesis 21:22 with a description of a blood covenant that the two men cut with each other. Abraham set seven ewe lambs of the flock by themselves "in order that it may be a witness to me" (Gen. 21:28, 30). "He called that place Beersheba: because there the two of them took an oath. So they made (***karath***) a covenant..." (vv. 31–32).

God was faithful in spite of Abraham's lack of faith. Once again, He rescued Abraham and Sarah from the consequences of Abraham's foolish, faithless decision. God came to Abimelech in a dream and said to him, "Behold, you are a dead man because of the woman whom you have taken, for she is married" (Gen. 20:3).

Abraham still had to learn that the faithfulness of God was not dependent on what he, Abraham, did or did not do. Neither did he need an obvious mark of covenant to show to those he encountered. Nor was God's faithfulness to protect him dependent on whether or not the other person knew that he was in a special relationship with the living God.

Abraham, like us, needed to learn that covenant with the Most High God is different from any other covenant. He is the Almighty God. He sees the secret places and knows the hidden things of man. And He is sovereign over the affairs of all men.

The Promised Son

The birth of Isaac must have been a time of great rejoicing. The curse of Sarah's barrenness was broken. Abraham finally had a son—the joy of his old age, the heir that would keep his name alive, the one promised of God to continue the covenant, and the fulfillment of all his hopes and dreams. Abraham's heart must have been overflowing with pride and wonder as he circumcised his son on the eighth day, thus fulfilling the ordinance of God and claiming the covenant promises for Isaac.[11]

The day Isaac was weaned, a great feast was held in celebration (v. 8). However, with rejoicing came conflict. Sarah saw Ishmael mocking* and became upset. "Therefore she said to Abraham, 'Drive out this maid and her son, for the son of this maid shall not be an heir with my son Isaac.' And the matter distressed Abraham greatly because of his son" (Gen. 21:9–11).

*Mocking is ***tsachaq***, which is the same word as "Isaac." (*Strong's*, H6711).

Ishmael had been Abraham's only son, his pride and joy for fourteen years. As his father, Abraham loved him and wanted the best for him.

> But God said to Abraham, "Do not be distressed because of the lad and your maid; whatever Sarah tells you, listen to her, for through Isaac your descendants shall be named. And of the son of the maid I will make a nation also, *because he is your descendant*." (Gen. 21:12–13, emphasis added)

The next morning, with heavy heart, Abraham gave Hagar and Ishmael bread and water and sent them out to wander in the barren desert. It seemed Abraham was sending them to a certain death, but God looked out for and protected them. He spoke directly with Hagar when she was distressed, and supernaturally provided food and water for Hagar and Ishmael in the wilderness. In time, the Lord made a great nation of Ishmael; even while knowing it would lead to centuries of conflict for His chosen people.[12]

Why did God bless Ishmael? Because Ishmael was a circumcised descendant of Abraham, and God honored the covenant with Abraham. It had nothing to do with Hagar and Ishmael. God had given Himself to Abraham and He was faithful to His promise—even when Abraham created complications by doing things in his own strength.

The Lord proved faithful again and again. He encouraged Abraham in his triumphs and did not forsake him when he failed. Consequently, Abraham grew in his understanding of who God was and of how to relate to Him. The relationship was no longer based on being afraid of displeasing a god. Abraham learned to trust his God in all things.

Abraham Gives His All

In Genesis 22, God gave Abraham a final test to prove him and see if he understood what it meant to be in a blood covenant relationship with the living God. Through this test, and Abraham's response, we can see more clearly what it means to walk in covenant with the Almighty God.

> The Lord "tested Abraham, and said to him, 'Abraham!'"
>
> Abraham immediately said, "Here I am."
>
> God said, "Take now your son, your only son, whom you love, Isaac, and go to the land of Moriah; and offer him there as a burnt offering on one of the mountains of which I will tell you." (Gen. 22:1–2)

Abraham obeyed immediately, without question or argument. He did not discuss his options with Sarah. Neither did he negotiate, as he had for Sodom and Gomorrah. He rose early the next morning, split wood for the burnt offering, and saddled his donkey. He took Isaac and two of his young men and went to the mountain as God instructed.

Abraham had waited years for the birth of his son in a society where it was devastating to not have an heir. Isaac was the delight of his life, his beloved son.* He was also the long-awaited miracle child prophesied by God, the one who would inherit all that God had promised. He was to be the seed for the mighty nation that would come from Abraham. Could God really expect him to take his son to present as a burnt offering?

*Isaac was not Abraham's only son. However, in Gen. 22:2, 12, and 16, as God is speaking to Abraham concerning the sacrifice, Isaac is referred to as "your only son." Isaac was the only begotten covenant son of Abraham and Sarah.

The Lord knew He was giving Abraham the ultimate challenge. He was asking for the one thing that was most dear to him. In obeying, Abraham would demonstrate understanding that his son belonged to his God. The Lord had been faithful to Abraham, but a blood covenant is a two-way agreement. It was time for Abraham to show his covenant faithfulness to God.

Abraham did not hesitate or question. The Most High God had asked for his son, and he trusted that God would provide a way.

It took several days to get to Moriah—several days for Abraham to think of the finality of sacrificing Isaac. Several days to reconsider his actions. However, "on the third day Abraham raised his eyes and saw the place from a distance. And Abraham said to his young men, 'Stay here with the donkey, and I and the lad will go yonder; and we will worship and return to you'" (Gen. 22:4–5).

How would you feel as you made the journey, knowing that God called you to sacrifice your beloved son on the mountain? We aren't told Abraham's feelings. However, his instructions to the young men who accompanied them were specific. Abraham trusted God.[13]

The two climbed the mountain. Abraham carried the fire and the knife. Isaac carried the wood for the burnt offering. As they ascended, there was probably tentativeness in Isaac's voice as he said, "*My father?*" (v. 7).

Abraham's response resonates with tenderness, "*Here am I, my son*" (v. 7).

Isaac continued, "Behold the fire and the wood: but where is the lamb for a burnt offering?" (v. 7).

"And Abraham said, 'God will provide for Himself the lamb for the burnt offering, my son.' So the two of them walked on together" (v. 8).

Abraham was confident. His words that "God would provide *for Himself* the lamb" are an indication that he knew his beloved son belonged to God.

But there was a problem. God's lamb was not evident when they reached the place of the sacrifice. Father and son were alone on the mountain.

Apparently without hesitation, he obeyed his God. He bound Isaac, laid him, his only beloved son, on the altar. The knife was raised. In Abraham's heart, Isaac was already sacrificed. He was already given to God. It was time to simply trust and obey—even if it meant sacrifice.

Abraham was confident the Lord would see to his need. There was no reason for him to protect what was his—God was his protection. There was no need to look for another sacrifice—God was his provision, his Jehovah Jireh. Abraham's reverence (fear) and love for God led him to surrender the thing closest to his heart.

Only then, as Abraham held the knife over Isaac, the angel of the Lord called to him out of heaven, "*Abraham, Abraham.*"

To Abraham's response, "Here I am," God said, "Do not stretch out your hand against the lad, and do nothing to him; *for now I know that you fear God, since you have not withheld your son, your only son, from Me*" (Gen. 22:12, emphasis added).

Everything Abraham had gone through in years past was preparation for this final test, and he passed. He obeyed immediately when God called him to go to Moriah and sacrifice his son. He left early in the morning without question. He took provision to make the sacrifice, and he answered his son's questions with confidence in his God. He did not waver in his obedience, but tied his son on the altar.

Because he did not withhold his son, his action proved that Abraham feared God.

All that Abraham had belonged to God, even his most prized possession. He was in covenant and would trust and obey, no matter what it cost him. By placing Isaac on the altar, he demonstrated that a blood covenant goes both ways. He revealed what it meant to walk in blood covenant with God.

As Abraham held the knife over his son, ready to sacrifice him, he looked up and saw a ram caught in the thicket by his horns. Abraham removed Isaac from the altar and offered the ram as a burnt offering in the place of his son. "Abraham named the place [Jehovah Jireh] The LORD Will Provide, as it is said to this day, 'In the mount of the LORD it will be provided'" (Gen. 22:14).

God continued by telling Abraham,

By Myself I have sworn, declares the LORD, *because you have done*

> *this thing, and have not withheld your son, your only son, indeed I will greatly bless you*, and I will greatly multiply your seed . . . and [they] shall possess the gate of their enemies. And in your seed all the nations of the earth shall be blessed, *because you have obeyed My voice*. (Gen. 22:16–18, emphasis added)

New Covenant Application

Just as Abraham was tested, we will be tested to see if we trust our God and if we have surrendered to Him. When the Lord asks for something precious, it seems like a loss to give it up. It feels like subtraction. However, as we surrender, we open the door to find God. He tests us in order to train us and to add to us.

Through trials we experience His faithfulness and gain understanding of Who He wants to be to us. God was patient and thorough in teaching Abraham what it meant to walk in covenant until he knew the nature of the relationship God desired with him.

As we undergo testing and seek God, we will find our faith and trust in Him maturing. Just as with Abraham, it will take time for us to be consistently confident that He is our protection and provision. Like Abraham, we need to learn that all we are and all we have belongs to our covenant-making, covenant-keeping God.

When Abraham gave his all, he found a ram waiting. Likewise, God has provided for us—Jesus is waiting for us to discover Him as our all in all. We will be tempted to hang on to what is precious to us. When we give it up, we will find God's provision and reward.

We will experience Him in His fullness only as we surrender our all to Him.

Chapter 3 Questions for Reflection and Discussion

1. What is most difficult for you to give up? When the Lord asks you to lay your "Isaac" on the altar, what will he/she/it look like?

2. Will you place your Isaac on the altar?

3. What did you learn about the nature and character of God through an overview of Abraham's life?

4. What did you learn from Abraham's spiritual journey?
   - In your life, what failures or lack of trust has God used to teach you to trust Him?
   - What successes has He used to confirm His presence and faithfulness?

5. Because Abraham felt God was slow to answer, Abraham took matters into his own hands to provide a son. It created immediate and long-lasting consequences for himself and others. When have you suffered consequences by moving ahead of God?

6. Read Proverbs 9:10. Abraham was told, "Now I know you fear God." Considering this verse and the life of Abraham and his relationship with God, define what it means to fear God.

Chapter 4

Abraham's Children

A blood covenant is passed from the father to his children down through the generations. Consequently, Abraham is just the beginning of the story of God's desire for an intimate relationship with His chosen people. The Lord said,

> Abraham will surely become a great and mighty nation, and in him all the nations of the earth will be blessed. For *I have chosen him, in order that he may command his children and his household after him to keep the way of the LORD* by doing righteousness and justice; in order that the LORD may bring upon Abraham what He has spoken about him. (Gen. 18:18–19, emphasis added)

God never intended that the intimate relationship with mankind end when Abraham died. He said, "For I have chosen him, *in order that* he may command his children" to do righteousness and justice (emphasis added).[1] The Lord's design from the beginning was for fathers and mothers to teach their children and households how to relate to Him in covenant. Therefore, it is the parents' responsibility to pass on faith.[2] What better way could children learn to fellowship with God and enjoy covenant blessings than through parents who knew and loved God?

The Lord is well aware of the sinful nature of mankind and our tendency to wander from Him. Therefore, in order to establish a solid foundation in covenant, He went beyond telling Abraham's son and grandson to teach their children. God confirmed the covenant with Isaac, with Jacob, and with the nation of Israel. He made sure they understood they were His covenant people. Many generations later, David spoke about the covenant being confirmed to his forefathers. He said,

> *Remember His covenant forever, the word which He commanded to a thousand generations,* the covenant which He made [karath, cut] *with Abraham*, and His oath *to Isaac*. He also confirmed it *to Jacob* for a statute, *to Israel* as an *everlasting* covenant, saying, "To you I will give the land of Canaan, as the portion of your inheritance." (1 Chron. 16:15–18, emphasis added)

The blood covenant is an everlasting covenant, passed down through the family. However, each generation needs its own personal relationship with the living God. They, in turn, teach their children and households to be faithful to the Lord and thus to the covenant He cut with Abraham.

There is a problem, however. Too often, commitment does not pass to the children, much less the grandchildren. Faith and fervor seem to wane with each generation. The challenge of passing on faith from one generation to another is evident in Abraham's family too—even though God came to Isaac and Jacob to reconfirm the covenant. A brief look at the generations following Abraham will illustrate how faith seemed to wane.

Isaac

We are not told how the patriarchs taught their children. However, there is evidence that Abraham sought to train Isaac. First, he circumcised his son at birth, thus fulfilling the covenant command and establishing Isaac's identity as one in covenant with the living God. We also know that Isaac was very obedient to his father, because as a young teen he allowed himself to be bound and placed on the altar as a sacrifice.*

*We assume Isaac was a teenager because in Genesis 22:12 when God told Abraham, "Do not stretch out your hand against the lad," the Hebrew word for lad is ***na'ar***, (Strongs, #5288), which means "a boy, from the age of infancy to adolescence." He appears to be an adolescent because he asked mature questions.

When it was time for Isaac to marry, Abraham took great care to keep his son from marrying a Canaanite woman. He sent his servant to Haran, to relatives, to find Isaac's mate. Abraham guarded what God had established. He did not let Isaac's marriage introduce an element that would compromise God's plan—that they be set apart and that they live in the land that God gave them.[3]

With Isaac, God was consistently faithful to the covenant, beginning with the provision of his wife. He supernaturally directed Abraham's servant to Rebekah. When she returned with the servant, Isaac took her as his wife "and it came about after the death of Abraham, that God blessed his son Isaac" (Gen. 25:11).

One testimony is recorded that shows Isaac had learned to seek the Lord. He sought God's help when in need. "Isaac prayed to the LORD on behalf of his wife, because she was barren; and the LORD answered him and Rebekah his wife conceived" (Gen. 25:21). Rebekah gave birth to twins, Esau and Jacob.

Later, during a famine, the Lord appeared to Isaac, telling him not to go down to Egypt. He told Isaac that if he stayed in the land of Canaan, that He would be with him and bless him and give the land to his descendants, "and I will *establish the oath* which *I swore [sevened myself]*** *to your father Abraham*" (Gen. 26:3). Furthermore, God repeated the promises made to Abraham, saying he would multiply Isaac's descendants as the stars, that He would give them the lands, and that by his "descendants all the nations of the earth shall be blessed; *because Abraham obeyed Me and kept My charge, My commandments, My statutes and My laws*" (Gen. 26:2–6, emphasis added).***

*Swear is *shaba'* (*Strong's*, H7650), means to seven oneself, or swear, "as if repeating a declaration seven times." It is the word that is used most often for swearing allegiance in a blood covenant, a seven-part ritual.

**These verses are often interpreted as the making of a new covenant, but several points confirm that it is the confirmation of the covenant cut with Abraham.

- The promises are the same as the promises to Abraham. God would not promise Isaac the same lands promised to Abraham if it were a separate covenant.
- "I will ***establish*** the oath" has the connotation that He will confirm or perform it. He will enact what He had promised, making it happen.
- God did these things, "***because Abraham obeyed Me and kept My charge***" (v. 5). Abraham's obedience would affect the covenant with Isaac only if it were the establishing of the same covenant.

As with Abraham, God spoke with Isaac personally. He not only gave specific directions, He also reaffirmed the covenant promises made to Abraham.

God Is Faithful

Unfortunately, children tend to inherit weaknesses as well as strengths from their parents. While in Gerar, Isaac demonstrated that each generation learns life's lessons for themselves. Isaac failed, just as his father had.

When the men asked about his wife, he told them, "She is my sister," for he was afraid to say, "my wife," thinking, "the men of the place might kill me on account of Rebekah, for she is beautiful" (Gen. 26:7).

Later, the Philistine king, Abimelech, looked out a window and saw Isaac caressing his Rebekah. Abimelech called Isaac and said, "Behold, certainly she is your wife! How then did you say, 'She is my sister'?"

> Isaac said, . . . "Because I said, 'Lest I die on account of her'" (Gen. 26:9).
>
> And Abimelech said, "What is this you have done to us? One of the people might easily have lain with your wife, and you would have brought guilt upon us." So Abimelech charged all the people, saying, "He who touches this man or his wife shall surely be put to death." (Gen. 26:9–11)

Abimelech not only forgave Isaac for his deceit, he also let Isaac's family settle in Gerar. Isaac planted crops and the Lord blessed him and he became rich until he was very wealthy, with many flocks and herds and many servants, leading the Philistines to envy him.

Finally, Isaac's great power seemed threatening, so Abimelech asked him to leave Gerar. However, even after he moved, Isaac continued to have conflict with the Philistines over wells that he dug.[4] He moved several times before he was far enough away that he found peace, after which Isaac acknowledged God for his good fortune. He said, "At last *the Lord has made room for us*, and we shall be fruitful in the land" (Gen. 26:22b, emphasis added).

Isaac then went up to Beersheba. That night the Lord appeared to him and said, "I am the God of your father Abraham; do not fear, for I am with you. I will bless you, and multiply your descendants, for the sake of My servant Abraham" (Gen. 26:24). Isaac responded by building an altar and worshiping the Lord. He also "pitched a tent, and his servants dug a well" (Gen. 26:25).

It is good to see that Isaac worshipped God, but why would scripture mention that he dug a well? Did Isaac plan to stay there? It seems significant that Isaac chose to remain in the place where God appeared and blessed him, particularly since Isaac was grateful to have found a different place where he could settle in peace.* Perhaps these verses demonstrate that Isaac's heart is responding to the Lord.

*Soon Abimelech asked Isaac to cut a covenant, because Isaac was blessed of God (Gen. 26:28–31).

Shortly before his death, Isaac confirmed understanding the covenant with God. After blessing Jacob, he added, "May He also give you the blessing of Abraham, to you and to your descendants with you; that you may possess the land of your sojournings, which God gave to Abraham" (Gen. 28:3–4).

Isaac learned from his father to acknowledge God, but we might question whether or not he developed the same kind of intimate relationship with God that Abraham had. The Lord remained faithful to guide, protect, and provide. However, as we will see, Isaac did not seem effective in leading his family in covenant faithfulness. His wife opposed him with deceit. His sons, Esau and Jacob, had difficulty getting along with each other and were both disappointing to him.

Jacob

When Rebekah was carrying the twins, the turmoil in her womb was so great that she sought the Lord. In response, God spoke to Rebekah and said, "Two nations are in your womb; and two peoples shall be separated from your body; and one people shall be stronger than the other; and the older shall serve the younger" (Gen. 25:23).

God's words to Rebekah were fulfilled. Twins were born to her and their relationship was fraught with strife. Esau was born first, "red, all over like a hairy garment." Jacob followed, "holding on to Esau's heel, so his name was called Jacob [one who takes by the heel, or supplants]; and Isaac was sixty years old when she gave birth to them" (Gen. 25:25–26).

Even at birth, Jacob seemed to be trying to gain advantage over Esau. However, continued trouble between the brothers may have been the result of something revealed in later verses. "When the boys grew up, Esau became a skillful hunter, a man of the field; but Jacob was a peaceful man, living in tents. Now *Isaac loved Esau*, because he had a taste for game; *but Rebekah loved Jacob*" (Gen. 25:27–28, emphasis added).

It often causes tension among siblings for a parent to show favoritism toward a particular child. In Isaac's family, it apparently split the family apart. It seems that jealousy over Isaac's favoritism toward Esau led to conflict. Whatever the root cause, Jacob seemed intent on gaining favor and was spurred on by his mother.

Traditionally, family names and titles, including the blessing, birthright, and line of covenant, passed down through the eldest son, enabling him to carry on as head of the family once the father died.[5] Esau, as first-born, would be the natural recipient of the birthright and blessing. However, one day . . .

> When Jacob had cooked stew, Esau came in from the field and he was famished; and Esau said to Jacob, "Please let me have a swallow of that red stuff there, for I am famished." . . .
>
> But Jacob said, "First sell me your birthright."
>
> And Esau said, "Behold, I am about to die; so of what use then is the birthright to me?"
>
> And Jacob said, "First swear to me"; so he swore to him, and sold his birthright to Jacob. Then Jacob gave Esau bread and lentil stew; and he ate and drank, and rose and went on his way. Thus Esau despised his birthright. (Gen. 25:29–34)

Jacob bargained with Esau to get his birthright and gained it with ease because Esau did not properly value it. Esau squandered his birthright in exchange for food to fill his stomach.

Robert and Kay: When our children were young, nearly every Sunday, a man in our church gave each of them a silver dollar after church. We appreciated his generosity, but didn't properly value the gift. We allowed them to spend some of the money on frivolous things. If we had guarded the silver dollars, they would have had real value when our children were older. The gift was squandered because we lacked appreciation. Perhaps this was how Esau managed to so easily give away his birthright; he didn't see the value at the time.

Isaac loved Esau, but it seems that his love was not fully returned. First of all, Esau did not value the birthright that was his through his father. He practically gave it away. Later it is recorded that he married Canaanites, women of his own choosing, not those that would please his father. The marriages were a serious issue because through the covenant of marriage, Esau became one with someone outside of the covenant with God. If he became head of the family, God's children would no longer be separate, set apart as the people of God.

In Genesis 26:35, we see that Esau's wives "brought grief to Isaac and Rebekah."

Blessed through Deception?

In spite of Esau's unfortunate choice of wives, he was in line to receive Isaac's blessing as the eldest son. When Isaac was old, his eyesight was failing, and he sensed death might be near. He called for Esau in preparation for blessing him. He said, "Please take your gear, your quiver and your bow, and go out to the field and hunt game for me; and prepare a savory dish for me such as I love, and bring it to me that I may eat, so that my soul may bless you before I die" (Gen. 27:3–4).

Rebekah listened carefully as Isaac gave Esau instructions, and then devised a scheme so Jacob could receive the blessing instead. She commanded Jacob to kill two young goats so she could make a savory dish for Isaac. Jacob could then take it to his father and thus receive Esau's blessing.

Jacob protested that his skin wasn't hairy like his brother's and said, "Perhaps my father will feel me, then I shall be as a deceiver in his sight; and I shall bring upon myself a curse and not a blessing" (Gen. 27:12). Notice that Jacob is not concerned about being deceptive, only about being caught in the deception and thereby cursed.

> But his mother said to him, "Your curse be on me, my son; only obey my voice, and go, get them for me."
>
> So he went and got them, and brought them to his mother; and his mother made savory food such as his father loved. Then Rebekah took the best garments of Esau her elder son, . . . and put them on Jacob her younger son. And she put the skins of the kids on his hands and on the smooth part of his neck. She also gave the savory food and the bread, which she had made, to her son Jacob.
>
> Then he came to his father and said, "My father."
>
> And he said, "Here I am. Who are you, my son?"
>
> And Jacob said to his father, "I am Esau your first-born; I have done as you told me. Get up, please, sit and eat of my game, that you may bless me." (Gen. 27:13–19)

Isaac continued to make inquiry and Jacob continued to lie in his answers. He said he was quick to bring the stew, "Because the LORD your God caused it to happen to me" (Gen. 27:20).

When Isaac asked to feel him to confirm that he was Esau, he was duped by the animal skin that Rebekah had covered Jacob's hand with. He said, "The voice is the voice of Jacob, but the hands are the hands of Esau." He then asked, "Are you really my son Esau?" (Gen. 27:20–24).

Once again, Jacob lied, "I am" (v. 24). Then Isaac took the food from Jacob and ate it. He had Jacob come close and kissed him.

Finally, when he smelled Jacob's garments, he noted that Jacob smelled like the outdoors, like a field. Then he blessed him.

> "Now may God give you of the dew of heaven, and of the fatness of the earth, and an abundance of grain and new wine; may peoples serve you, and nations bow down to you; be master of your brothers, and may your mother's sons bow down to you. Cursed be those who curse you, and blessed be those who bless you." (Gen. 27:27b–29)

Shortly after Jacob left Isaac's presence, Esau returned. He brought savory food to his father as Isaac had instructed. Jacob's deception was exposed. When Isaac heard Esau's words, he trembled violently and said, "Who was he then that hunted game and brought it to me, so that I ate of all of it before you came, and blessed him? Yes, and he shall be blessed" (Gen. 27:33).

In anguish and bitterness, Esau cried, "Bless me, even me also, O my father!" (Gen. 27:34).

Isaac said, "Your brother came deceitfully, and has taken away your blessing" (Gen. 27:35).

Esau said, "Is he not rightly named Jacob, for he has supplanted me these two times? He took away my birthright, and behold, now he has taken away my blessing." He then pleaded with Jacob, "Don't you have a blessing for me?" (Gen. 27:36).

But Isaac answered and said to Esau, "Behold, I have made him your master, and all his relatives I have given to him as servants; and with grain and new wine I have sustained him. Now as for you then, what can I do, my son?" (Gen. 27:37).

Isaac did not have a blessing for his eldest son, the one he loved. He had already given it to Jacob. Instead of a blessing, he told Esau,

> "Behold, away from the fertility of the earth shall be your dwelling, and away from the dew of heaven from above. and by your sword you shall live, and your brother you shall serve; but it shall come about when you become restless, that you shall break his yoke from your neck." (Gen. 27:39–40)

Esau was understandably angry. He threatened that he would kill his younger brother as soon as his father died. Jacob had to flee from his family.[6]

Jacob Leaves Home

Isaac directed Jacob's flight. He sent him to Paddan-aran, to the house of Laban, Rebekah's brother. There Jacob could find a wife among kin. Like

Abraham, Isaac chose for Jacob to marry a relative so they could remain a separate people.*

*After Esau saw that his parents didn't approve of his Hittite marriages, he married a daughter of Ishmael (Gen. 28:8–9).

While gaining the prized birthright and blessing, Jacob did not exhibit faith in a covenant God to work on his behalf. He had earned his name, "One Who Supplants." He manipulated, deceived, and lied to obtain both the birthright and the blessing. He knew he didn't deserve them. He probably felt guilty. As he traveled alone toward Haran, he was likely reliving the events of his deception. He had blown it with his family and probably with God. What would happen to him now?

Jacob needed reassurance in order to develop a trusting relationship with the Lord. As always, God took the initiative to build that bond. He answered Jacob's need.

Jacob stopped on the roadside to rest for the night. He put a rock under his head as he lay down to sleep. Though weary from the journey, Jacob dreamed as he slept. He saw a ladder that reached from earth into the heavens. Angels were climbing up and down the ladder. The Lord stood above it and repeated the covenant blessings given to Abraham, promising to give the land to Jacob and his descendants, that his descendants would be like the dust, that his offspring would spread out in all directions, and that in him and his descendants all the families of the earth would be blessed. Furthermore, God told him, "And behold, I am with you, and will keep you wherever you go, and will bring you back to this land; for I will not leave you until I have done what I have promised you" (Gen. 28:13–15).

God reassured Jacob. Even as he was running for his life, God repeated the covenant blessings, personalizing them for Jacob. He emphasized His commitment with, "I am with you and will keep you wherever you go. I will bring you back to this land and will not leave you." Jacob was given full assurance that he was part of the covenant blessings promised to Abraham—even though he gained the birthright and blessing through deceit.

When Jacob awoke from the dream, he said, "Surely the Lord is in this place, and I did not know it. How awesome is this place! This is none other than the house of God, and this is the gate of heaven" (Gen. 28:16–17). Jacob then made a vow, saying:

> "*If God* will be with me and will keep me . . . and will give me food to eat and garments to wear, *and I return to my father's house in safety, then the Lord will be my God.* And this stone, which I

have set up as a pillar, will be God's house; and of all that Thou dost give me I will surely give a tenth to Thee." (Gen. 28:20–22, emphasis added)

Before this point, Jacob was in charge of his life. He had not embraced God as *his* God. Through deceit, he had gotten what he wanted—but it cost him everything he had known. He had to leave his home and family and dwell in a strange land. However, because of the covenant, God promised to be with him and to bless him.

In return, Jacob made a conditional promise to recognize the Lord as his God *if* God would do certain things to provide for and protect him. One of those conditions was that he would someday return to his father's house. Jacob was at least forty years old when he left home and it would be twenty years before he returned. If—as a forty-year-old—he made a commitment to recognize the Lord as his God only if his conditions were met, we might conclude that Jacob did not learn to love the God of his fathers as a child. From this point on, he seemed to be a man of integrity. However, there is no indication that his heart turned to God until he was about sixty years old and returning to the home of his father.

In Haran, God led Jacob to Laban, who welcomed him as family. Jacob worked for Laban for seven years to earn the right to marry his daughter Rachel, whom he loved. But Laban tricked Jacob and gave him Leah as a wife instead. Jacob had to work seven more years in order to wed Rachel.[7] Fierce rivalry developed between Leah and Rachel because Rachel was loved but barren, and Leah, who was unloved, had many sons for Jacob.

After God opened her womb and Joseph was born to Rachel, Jacob asked Laban if he could go home. But Laban did not want Jacob to leave. He said, "I have learned by divination that the LORD has blessed me because of you" (Gen. 30:27 NIV). However, difficulties with Laban continued to escalate.[8] Finally, while Rachel was pregnant with Benjamin, God told Jacob to return home. He sneaked away without telling Laban.*

*Genesis 31:20. Laban chased after Jacob. God intercepted him and told him not to say anything to Jacob. When he caught up with him, they cut a covenant as a witness between them to guarantee no harm would come to him or his daughters and grandchildren (Genesis 31:43–55).

Jacob's Return Home

As Jacob traveled home, he feared meeting Esau. He finally came to the end of himself and his ability to handle things. He cried out to his covenant God and declared that he was unworthy of the Lord's loving kindness* and faithfulness toward him. He also prayed for deliverance from his brother, where he would find certain wrath.[9]

*Loving kindness (*checed, Strong's*, H2617) refers to God's mercy, kindness, and faithfulness, which proceeds from covenant. Appendix E explains the covenant significance of *checed* (also spelled *hesed*).

Again, the Lord met Jacob in the night. He wrestled with him until daybreak.

> Then He said, "Let me go, for the dawn is breaking."
>
> But [Jacob] said, "I will not let you go unless you bless me."
>
> So He said to him, "What is your name?"
>
> And he said, "Jacob."
>
> And He said, "Your name shall no longer be Jacob, but Israel; for you have striven with God and with men and have prevailed."
>
> Then Jacob asked Him and said, "Please tell me your name."
>
> But He said, "Why is it that you ask my name?" And He blessed him there.
>
> So Jacob named the place Peniel, for he said, "I have seen God face to face, yet my life has been preserved." (Gen. 32:26–30)

Later, Jacob's daughter Dinah was defiled, and Jacob was slow to do anything about it. His sons took revenge and killed all the men in the city where the assault had occurred. Jacob was afraid of retaliation from other tribes. Consequently, he once again looked to his God for help.

The Lord came to him and said, "Arise, go up to Bethel, and live there; and make an altar there to God, who appeared to you when you fled from your brother Esau" (Gen. 35:1). Jacob not only built an altar, he commanded his household to get rid of foreign gods, to purify themselves, and change their garments.

It seems Jacob finally chose to trust in God rather than himself. He also took leadership in his family to turn them toward the Lord. Immediately after the sacrifice, God appeared to Jacob again. The Lord changed his name from Jacob (one who supplants) to Israel (he will rule as God), and repeated the promises made to Abraham.

When Jacob returned home, he was received by Esau and lived in Canaan, where God blessed him with abundance.* In time, a famine forced Jacob to move to Egypt for food.

*Jacob was recognized as head of the family. When it became too crowded for them to live together, Esau moved and left Jacob in Canaan as the one in line for the covenant blessings (Gen. 36:7–8).

Jacob's Sons

Jacob's sons give further evidence that as a young father, Jacob did not have a vital relationship with God or train his children to love the Lord. Jacob's older sons did not live righteously or show understanding of covenant. We see this first when Jacob was traveling home with his family, and his daughter Dinah—as we mentioned earlier—was defiled by Hamor. Hamor and his father then asked for Dinah's hand in marriage.

Jacob's sons replied that the only way he could marry Dinah would be if the men became circumcised.** The whole city agreed and every male was circumcised. However, on the third day, when the men were incapacitated with pain, Jacob's sons Simeon and Levi attacked. They killed all the men and looted the city of wealth, cattle, women, and children.[10] In their dealings with Hamor, Jacob's sons did not show any recognition of God, much less honor Him as God.

**This seems to be a demand that they cut covenant together if the city wanted to become part of Israel, but it is not conclusive.

Years later, when younger brother Joseph was seventeen years old, the older brothers became jealous because their father favored him. Joseph went to them in the field where they were tending sheep. Their jealousy was so great that they faked his death, sold him to traders to be a slave, and reported him to their father as dead. If Reuben and Judah had not stood up in his defense, he would have been killed.

Scripture gives little evidence that Jacob's sons feared God or walked in righteousness. Nor did they seem to understand the covenant. After Abraham, the covenant seemed to grow weaker with each generation. The one exception is Joseph, the son of Rachel, the wife whom Jacob loved. Even though Joseph's brothers hated him and sold him into slavery, he exemplified godly behavior in the midst of mistreatment and hardship.*

*Joseph's life demonstrates covenant understanding that is not evident in the lives of his older brothers. He had a great capacity for trusting God, for forgiving those who wronged him, and for serving with abundant grace. Joseph:

· Had God-inspired visions of the future as a young lad (Gen. 37:5–10);

· Served with excellence as a slave (Gen. 39:2–4) after being sold by jealous brothers (Gen. 37:11–26);

· Maintained moral standards when his master's wife tried to seduce him (Gen. 39:5–20);

· Served with excellence when imprisoned on false charges (Gen. 39:20–23);

· Heard from God the interpretation of Pharaoh's dreams (Gen. 40–41:36);

· Served with wisdom and excellence as second to Pharaoh (Gen. 41:37–57); and

· Forgave his brothers for their treachery towards him, stating that God had a purpose in it and meant it for good (Gen. 42–45, specifically 45:5–9, Gen. 50:20).

The Nation of Israel

While Joseph was in Egypt and in prison as a slave, God gave him interpretations to Pharaoh's dreams. Consequently, he was taken from prison and given a place of prominence in Egypt.[11] When his brothers came to Egypt for food during the famine, he was in power. He invited his family to come live in Egypt. They multiplied rapidly, and Israel's twelve sons became the heads of the twelve tribes of the nation Israel.[12] A new king was threatened by their numbers and enslaved the whole nation.[13]

We have seen that Joseph's brothers did not seem to know the Lord and certainly didn't fear Him. Consequently, they could not pass a strong faith to their children. Not surprisingly their descendents, the Israelites, did not seem to understand their covenant relationship with the living God. Although God blessed and preserved them because of His covenant with Abraham, they were slaves in Egypt for four hundred years before they cried out to God for help.

New Covenant Application of an Everlasting Covenant

In spite of the short-comings of Abraham's descendants, the Lord remained covenantly faithful in their lives. He also maintained a remnant who honored Him. The Lord will always be faithful to the covenant. And yet, He calls His children to be faithful too.

As is evident in Abraham's offspring, being born into an everlasting covenant does not automatically ingrain faith in children. Even if God personally confirms the covenant to each, succeeding generations are not guaranteed a vital relationship with the Lord. The same is true today. God has given parents responsibility to train their children to walk in covenant. Unless God miraculously intervenes, if parents do not teach their children to love, trust, and obey Him, following generations tend to slip further and further from God.

When things are going well, it's easy to forget that all of our blessings are a gift from God. He said, "*Give heed to yourself and keep your soul diligently, lest you forget the things which your eyes have seen*, and lest they depart from your heart all the days of your life; but make *them known to your sons and your grandsons*" (Deut. 4:9, emphasis added). Parents need to guard their own hearts as well as train their children, because you can't pass on what you don't have yourself.

Parenting is one of the most important jobs we have, and a central part of the task is to lead our children to a personal relationship with Jesus Christ so they will love, fear, and obey Him all of their days. In Deuteronomy 6, the Lord reiterated the command for "you and your son and your grandson" to obey the commandments of the Lord "all the days of your life . . . that it may be well with you and that you may multiply greatly, just as the LORD, the God of your fathers, has promised you, in a land flowing with milk and honey" (Deut. 6:1–3). The phrase, "God of your fathers," reminds us that the God of promise is in covenant with us and He is loving, merciful, kind, and covenantly faithful to us as we seek to follow His commands.

The next verses emphasize the beginning point for parents who want their children to walk in covenant faithfulness and blessings. "You shall love the LORD your God with all your heart and with all your soul and with all your might. And these words, which I am commanding you today, shall be on your heart" (Deut. 6:5–6).

How can we teach our children to walk in an intimate covenant relationship with God if we do not model it for them? We need to teach them to know the Word of God, and share stories of His faithfulness in our lives, but if our walk with our Lord is not authentic, it will undermine the things we try to teach.

Children are a gift, an inheritance, a reward from the Lord (Ps. 127:3). Likewise, because we are in covenant relationship with God and all we have belongs to Him, our children are His too. We are not alone in the challenging job of training them. He is with us. However, that does not minimize our responsibility to obey His command that we train our children.

Our greatest challenge may be remembering our covenant partner so we don't try to do the job on our own. We cannot fully know or shape our children's hearts. As we call out to the Lord, it is His job to form their hearts, or to transform them if that is the need.

"If your sons keep my covenant and the statutes I teach them, then their sons will sit on your throne for ever and ever" (Ps. 132:12 NIV). "For the eyes of the LORD move to and fro throughout the earth that He may strongly support those whose heart is completely His" (2 Chr. 16:9).

Chapter 4 Questions for Reflection and Discussion

1. Rebekah intervened to make sure Jacob received the blessing from Isaac in Esau's place (Genesis 27). Do you think she was pleased with the outcome/consequences of her actions?
   - Why, and why not?
   - What did you learn from Rebekah?

2. Read Deuteronomy 6. In these verses, we are told to love, fear, and obey God and to teach our children to do so. (Fear is *yare,* the word used when God told Abraham, "now I know you fear God" in Gen. 22:12).
   - Who is responsible for teaching children?
   - Where/when are we to teach our children?
   - What rewards are mentioned for following God's commands in Deuteronomy 6?
     i. (v. 2)
     ii. (v. 3)
     iii. (v. 3)
     iv. (v. 10–11)
     v. (v. 24)
     vi. (v. 24)
     vii. (v. 25)
   - What are we to guard against?

3. What are the secrets to training children who are strong in the Lord?
   - What can we learn from the characteristics of our heavenly Father?
   - What makes it so difficult to predict the outcome of your own parenting?
   - Verses to gain further insight: Psalms 78:5,Psalms 132:12, Proverbs 22:6, Proverbs 22:6, Malichi 4:6, Matthew 28:19–20, Ephesians 6:4, Colossians 3:21, Hebrews 12:6-12, .

Chapter 5

Moses Learns That God Is With Him

Jacob's children became known as the nation of Israel, after the new name given to Jacob by God. They multiplied so rapidly while in Egypt that the new pharaoh feared their numbers and made them slaves. Later, as they continued to multiply, a command went out that all male newborns be killed. Moses was born during that edict. However, God miraculously saved him and he was reared in the household of Pharaoh—until Moses killed an Egyptian and had to flee for his life. He fled to the land of Midian and lived as a shepherd, caring for the sheep of his father-in-law.[1]

The Call of Moses

All Scriptural accounts of Midian, except that they received Moses as one of them, indicate that they were hostile to Israel. Apparently, while in exile, Moses had no fellowship with other believers. nothing to encourage him in his faith. He was hiding, minding his own business, and faithfully doing his job.

While tending sheep, he saw a burning bush that was not consumed. It is not unusual for thorn bushes in that region to ignite spontaneously and burn with a loud crackle, but they quickly burn out.[2] This bush was not consumed, so Moses turned to investigate.[3]

"The Lord saw that he turned aside to look. God called to him from the midst of the bush" (Ex. 3:4a). Moses apparently did not realize it was

God until a voice spoke from the bush, and said, "Do not come near here; remove your sandals from your feet, for the place on which you are standing is holy ground." He also said, "I am the God of your father, the God of Abraham, the God of Isaac, and the God of Jacob" (Ex. 3:5–6). Moses responded by hiding his face because he was afraid to look at God.

In our first glimpse of the relationship between Moses and God, Moses feared the God of his fathers and showed Him reverence. Then God gave him an assignment:

> Behold, the cry of the sons of Israel has come to Me; furthermore, I have seen the oppression with which the Egyptians are oppressing them. Therefore, come now, and I will send you to Pharaoh, so that you may bring My people, the sons of Israel, out of Egypt. (Ex. 3:10)

Moses had many questions and uncertainties that would make it difficult to return to Egypt. Forty years had passed while Moses was in exile. Many things would have changed. He had been part of the royal family, but God was asking him to return as a representative of his people, the slaves. Would his family still be alive? Would his people receive him? Would the new pharaoh seek to kill him? While we don't know Moses' thoughts, we can understand that he might not be eager to obey God's call to return to Egypt and go to Pharaoh to seek the release of God's children.

We returned to our former home town after six years and were able to visit with a group of church friends from the past. It wasn't like it used to be. Many of them were attending different churches, with new circles of friends. The sense of oneness had vanished. Think how different life would be in Egypt after forty years. Life moves on.

Moses wouldn't have friends to return to because he had been part of the royal family. As a murderer, he would not be welcomed by the Egyptians. In fact, Moses would probably be imprisoned, if not killed. How could he lead God's people out? He said, "Who am I, that I should go to Pharaoh, and that I should bring the sons of Israel out of Egypt?" (Ex. 3:11).

Moses had been a misfit since his birth. He was reared as an Egyptian, but he was not one of them—he was a Hebrew, with the heart of a Hebrew. He had lived in opulence—served by his kin, royalty—who chose to identify with slaves.

As the adopted son of Pharaoh, Moses might have been able to help his people. However, in one impetuous moment, he squandered everything.

He murdered an Egyptian and became a fugitive. Now, neither Egyptians nor Israelites would trust him.

For forty years, Moses lived among the Midianites caring for his father-in-law's sheep. As a shepherd, he held the lowest rank in the society. And he was not a Midianite. He was in exile, a foreigner.[4] How could God want him?

"Who am I?" It was a valid question. Moses was a nobody. A misfit. A failure. A murderer.

It seemed God did not hear Moses' question, but He answered it anyway. In effect, God told Moses, "It doesn't matter about you, about who you are, what you've done, or about your problems. It's all about Me."

God said, "*Certainly I will be with you*, and this shall be the sign to you that it is I who have sent you: when you have brought the people out of Egypt, you shall worship God at this mountain" (Ex. 3:12, emphasis added). "I will be with you. You and I are one. In your weakness, My strength will be made known. You can trust in Me. '*Certainly, I will be with you*'" (Ex. 3:12, emphasis added).

The Lord called Moses to faith by giving him a mission that was too big for him. With the mission, God promised that the whole nation of Israel would worship Him at the mountain. The picture of his people at the mountain worshipping in freedom would confirm the calling and motivate Moses to persevere through the challenges ahead.

In essence, God told him, "Trust Me. Obey. Lead My people. And this is a sign for you: you will worship Me on this mountain—accompanied by millions of people—your family—free."

Moses hesitated and questioned God. It is clear in his question that he is considering going to Egypt. He seemed to be thinking, "OK, it's not about me, it's about You. But who *are* You?" He questioned God, "Behold, I am going to the sons of Israel, and I shall say to them, 'The God of your fathers has sent me to you.' Now they may say to me, 'What is His name?' What shall I say to them?" (Ex. 3:13).

"I AM WHO I AM," said God, "Thus you shall say to the sons of Israel, I AM has sent me to you" (from Ex. 3:14).

God is the self-existent One, the source of life, and of all created things. He is the One who had being before there was being.[5] He is the same yesterday, today, and forever. Inherent in this name is the unchanging character of the living God who chose to be one with Israel.[6]

As if that were not enough, God continued, "Thus you shall say to the sons of Israel, 'The LORD, the God of your fathers, the God of Abraham, the God of Isaac, and the God of Jacob, has sent me to you.' This is My name forever, and this is My memorial name to all generations" (Ex. 3:15).

God did not stop with a description and name that declared His omnipotence. He personalized His identity with Israel: "the God of your fathers," of Abraham, Isaac, and Jacob. He wanted His children to hear "I am *your* God. You are *My* people." He used covenant talk to help them understand, to begin stirring something deep in their hearts that had gone dormant during their time of slavery. The Israelites needed to hear this.

But first Moses needed to hear. Forty years earlier, he had a vision of freeing his people from their cruel bondage, but it was thwarted when he killed a taskmaster. His vision died on the back of the desert. God had to first convince Moses that he was the man for the job, and that what he lacked, the Lord would provide. Moses needed to know that God would be with him.

Next, Moses questioned the Lord about his stammering speech. God was patient. He told Moses, "Now then go, and *I, even I, will be with your mouth,* and teach you what you are to say" (Ex. 4:12, emphasis added). God was saying, "Moses, where you are weak, I will be with you. Whatever you need, I will be there—even with your mouth."

Moses still wanted someone else to be the messenger. God became angry,[7] but He met Moses in his lack of faith. He assigned Aaron as spokesman, telling Moses, "And you are to speak to him and put the words in his mouth; and *I, even I, will be with your* mouth and his mouth, and I will teach you what you are to do" (Ex. 4:15, emphasis added).

Moses Journeys to Egypt

Moses finally relented and began the journey to Egypt. However, not surprisingly, it took time for Moses to learn what it meant that God would be with him. His first hurdle was an encounter with God. Moses stopped for the night and "the Lord met him and sought to put him to death."

> Then Zipporah [Moses' wife] took a flint and cut off her son's foreskin and threw it at Moses' feet, and she said, "You are indeed a bridegroom of blood to me." So He let him alone. At that time she said, "You are a bridegroom of blood"— because of the circumcision. (Ex. 4:24–26)

At first glance, this scene does not make sense. After the trouble to get him to go to Egypt, why would God try to kill Moses before he had a chance to begin his mission? And why would Zipporah see her husband struggling for his life and respond by circumcising their son?

Why? Because either Zipporah understood the problem, or Moses understood and told her what to do—and her actions reveal why God attacked Moses.

It dealt with the circumcision of their son.

God had told Abraham, "But an uncircumcised male who is not circumcised in the flesh of his foreskin, that person shall be cut off [*karath*] from his people; he has broken My covenant" (Gen. 17:14). There were consequences for ignoring circumcision. Moses broke a basic covenant command. He had been circumcised as a baby but he failed to circumcise his youngest son.[8] God was cutting Moses off for breaking covenant by ignoring circumcision.*

*Moses was held responsible for the circumcision even though the reason he chose not to circumcise his son was apparently because of Zipporah's abhorrence of the procedure.

If Moses was not being obedient, how could God release him to lead His children back to the Promised Land?[9] Moses could not intercede on behalf of God's covenant people if he was not rightly relating to God as a covenant member himself. The Lord confronted Moses in order to bring him into compliance. As soon as Zipporah had performed the circumcision, God released Moses and his life was spared.

Moses Confronts the Pharaoh

Meanwhile, God sent Aaron to meet Moses.[10] Together they traveled back to Egypt and went before Pharaoh.

Pharaoh had a problem. He did not know the living God. Neither did he know that God had promised to fight for His children. Pharaoh was accustomed to being the most powerful man on earth. He didn't realize he was opposing a foe that was stronger than himself, his army, his magicians, and his gods all put together. He was confident that he would win, because he didn't know the God above all gods had promised to be with Moses.

Even after Egypt was devastated by nine plagues, each proclaiming victory over Egypt's false gods, Pharaoh refused to release Israel. Instead, he continued to increase their workload, making the lives of the slaves even more miserable. Interestingly, several times scripture tells us that *God* hardened Pharaoh's heart.[11]

Why would God harden his heart? After all, He knew it would lead to more suffering for Israel. Did the Lord intentionally prolong His children's agony by causing a more difficult workload?

In Exodus 7:3, God tells us that He wanted to show His "signs and wonders in the land of Egypt" so the Egyptians would know He is the Lord.[12] But the signs didn't seem to impress the Egyptians. Nor did they hasten the release of Israel. So, why would God prolong agony for His chosen people just to multiply signs and wonders?

Consider another question. Who, besides the Egyptians, saw the miracles of God?

The Israelites. The signs introduced God to His children. After being oppressed their whole lives, the children of Israel were told *their* God was concerned about them, had seen their affliction,[13] and sent a deliverer. As they observed the might and power of God, they grew in knowledge of who their God was and gained hope for the first time in generations. Through unprecedented signs and wonders wrought by Him on *their* behalf, they experienced first-hand what a mighty God they had.

The miracles impacted Moses too. When he arrived in Egypt, he had no faith in himself and little faith in God. Even though the Lord told Moses that He would be with him, Moses was not yet confident in God. The greatest impact of the plagues on Egypt may have been on Moses.

Step-by-step Moses obeyed God and did just as he was told.[14] And the Lord continued to do miraculous things. The Lord God Almighty worked through Moses to cause water to turn to blood, frogs and flies to invade, and disease and boils to molest. Moses knew it was not him doing those things. He did not have such power. With each plague and each encounter with Pharaoh, Moses learned with greater certainty that God was almighty, was faithful, and was with him.

Moses learned, too, that God was available when he had a request. Once, rather than call off the frogs, Moses allowed Pharaoh to designate the time of the departure. The next day, Moses cried out to God asking Him to remove the frogs. "And the LORD did according to the word of Moses, and the frogs died out" (Ex. 8:9–13). God is sovereign, but He recognized Moses as a partner in the process. Day by day and plague by plague, Moses grew in his understanding of what it meant for God to be *with* him.

Moses and the Israelites were finally released after the death angel killed the eldest son in each Egyptian household. It took the death of Pharaoh's firstborn before he was convinced to let Israel go. The death angel passed over the homes of Israel, sparing them, because of the blood covenant and because God's children obeyed and sprinkled blood over each door.

Free at Last

Six hundred thousand men with their wives and children, plus their flocks and herds, snaked their way out of Egypt. They were a strong people, strengthened by forced labor. All they had known was cruel slavery. Suddenly, they were free. They carried payment for four hundred years of work: gifts of gold, silver, and fine clothing that the Egyptians piled on them as they left.[15] They must have been wide-eyed with excitement and wonder as they began their freedom journey.

However, the Lord did not just release His children, free to go on their way. He *led* them out of bondage. He appeared in a cloud, which shielded them from the sun in the day, and a pillar of fire, which gave them light at night.[16] God led them away from Egypt and through the wilderness. Rather than following the shortest route, they passed through a valley between two high mountain ridges, and then paused to camp on a beach by the Red Sea.

Faith Versus Fear

Before they had time to settle, those in the rear heard a distant rumble. No doubt, when they looked back, they saw dust billowing in the wind—dust from charging chariots. The Egyptians were coming after them!

Word spread quickly. Terror and confusion erupted. A great sea was before them, towering mountains beside them, and a vicious army overtaking them. There was no escape. How could they stand against the Egyptians? In their terror, they cried out to God for help.

> Then they said to Moses, "Is it because there were no graves in Egypt that you have taken us away to die in the wilderness? Why have you dealt with us in this way, bringing us out of Egypt? Is this not the word that we spoke to you in Egypt, saying, 'Leave us alone that we may serve the Egyptians'? For it would have been better for us to serve the Egyptians than to die in the wilderness." (Ex. 14:10–12)

The Israelite's cry to God proved their knowledge of Him. However, they did not cry out in faith. Instead, they visualized calamity. Immediately after crying out to God, they blamed Moses for leading them to sure death. They wished for continued slavery rather than to be overtaken by the Egyptians. Knowledge of God—even first-hand knowledge of His power and might—did not produce faith in Israel when they faced a crisis.

Application: Few of us have been chased by an army, but many have felt hopelessly trapped, sure that catastrophe is inevitable and doom certain. Difficult family circumstances, broken relationships, failing health, or financial burdens can lead to fear or a sense of helplessness. Like Israel, when we feel trapped and helpless, we tend to visualize calamity and cast blame on others—even while crying out to God.

The Israelites were afraid, and with reason. They knew first-hand about the might and cruelty of the approaching foe. They did not have the skill, weapons, or courage, to stand against such a vicious enemy.

Israel was trapped, caught between two fronts—the approaching army and the terrified, complaining multitude who blamed *Moses* for their troubles.

What could Moses do?

Unlike the multitude, Moses stood—and his words rang with faith. "Do not fear! Stand by and see the salvation of the LORD which He will accomplish for you today; for the Egyptians whom you have seen today, you will never see them again forever. The LORD will fight for you while you keep silent" (Ex. 14:13–14).

In the midst of the crisis, Moses boldly proclaimed, "Do not fear!" After walking with the Lord through the plagues, he was confident in the power of God. What was there to fear? Had God not promised to be with them and be their shield?

Moses had changed. Unlike the man at the burning bush in Midian who was afraid to return to Egypt, he was now willing to stand against the mighty Egyptian army.

The Israelites and Moses both cried out to God when the army approached. However, the multitude were terrified, and their words were filled with fear, blame, and doom. They looked at the approaching army and visualized attack and certain death.

In contrast, Moses looked at his covenant-keeping God and trusted Him for protection. He recognized the threat, but, instead of picturing slaughter, Moses hoped in the God of Israel. Moses cried out in faith.

"The mouth speaks out of that which fills the heart" (Matt. 12:34). "Faith is the substance of things hoped for, the evidence of things not seen" (Heb. 11:1 KJV). Moses' faith gained substance through seeing God's faithfulness throughout the plagues in Egypt. That concrete foundation of trust in a covenant-keeping God gave Moses faith and courage to say, "Fear not."

Moses' words also gave needed direction. When overwhelmed by fear, it is hard to know what to do. Moses called Israel to look beyond their fears. He spoke with confidence as he said, "Stand by [stand still] and see the salvation of the LORD which He will accomplish for you today."[17] His direction was clear, "Quit moaning and crying. Stop looking at the Egyptians. Stand still. Look at the Lord."

The word for *stand by* or *stand still* is *yatsab*.[18] It means "to place or station one's self." The first time it is used in the Bible is when Miriam watched over the infant Moses as he lay among the bulrushes. "And his sister stood [*yatsab*] at a distance to find out what would happen to him" (Ex. 2:4).

Yatsab doesn't imply that we stop all activity when we stand still. We are to take a stand, to station ourselves, where we can see what is about to happen. Standing, we watch expectantly, waiting for the Lord to act. If we don't position ourselves to see, we might miss the Lord's salvation.

Moses called Israel to change their focus. Stop gaping at the approaching chariots. Instead, gaze upon the always-faithful living God—*their* God.

If we lean on God as our covenant partner, His purposes will be accomplished. When He takes care of something, it is settled. Moses said, "for the Egyptians whom you have seen today, you will *never* see them again *forever*" (emphasis added). That is quite a promise.

Imagine being a slave, and all you've known is slavery. You're trapped at the Red Sea. The army is closing in. You know the end is near. You have no weapons—and don't know how to use them anyway. Your vicious oppressors are rapidly approaching. Then, in the midst of the chaos, Moses proclaims that you will *never* see the foe again—*forever*!

And Moses was right.*

*If we trust in God as our covenant partner, His purposes will be accomplished, but that does not guarantee us a trouble free life. Under the Old Covenant, there were consequences/curses for disobedience and unfaithfulness. In the New Covenant, that is also true. However, "all who desire to live godly in Christ Jesus" are promised that we will "be persecuted for the sake of righteousness" (2 Tim. 3:12, Matt. 5: 10–12). Just as Jesus was persecuted, we can expect to be persecuted if we are in Him. We can rejoice in our suffering because through it we are purified, strengthened, and grow in grace in Him.

The Lord Will Fight for You

The essence of walking in the blessing of covenant protection is summed up in Exodus 14:14, "The Lord will fight for you *while you keep silent*" (emphasis added) or "The Lord will fight for you and *you will hold your peace*" (KJV, emphasis added). If the Israelites had known the greatness of God's power and the plans He had for defeating the Egyptians, there would be no need to panic, murmur, and blame. Instead, they would have waited and watched with quiet, peaceful, excitement, waiting to see how God would defeat an army.

But, one might argue, they knew God's power. They had seen it in Egypt as He destroyed a mighty nation with one plague after another. Yes, they had experienced His miraculous power first hand. However, they didn't know His plan to get them out of their predicament. It looked impossible. Besides, they were just slaves. They were nobodies. Why would God do anything for them?

Moses had learned his lesson. He knew without a doubt that God was with him—and that He would fight for Israel. Moses' faith was not misplaced. God *was* with Israel.

The Lord told Moses, "Why are you crying out to Me? Tell the sons of Israel to go forward. And as for you, lift up your staff and stretch out your hand over the sea and divide it, and the sons of Israel shall go through the midst of the sea on dry land" (Ex. 14:15–16).

Why did God ask Moses to lift up his staff? In battle, what does it mean when hands are lifted up? Is it not a sign of surrender? In our relationship with God, we worship Him through lifting holy hands. Moses' lifted hand acknowledges the Lord and Moses' dependence on Him.

It was not just a stick that Moses held up. Moses staff: (1) symbolized authority, as the scepter would for a king, (2) was carried in his right hand, the hand that stood for power and authority, and (3) was a necessary tool for a shepherd to do his job. (4) The rod was also the instrument God told him to carry for performing the signs.[19] As Moses lifted his staff heavenward, he yielded everything to God—his power, authority, and livelihood. By raising his staff, Moses surrendered everything to God and acknowledged his dependence on Him.

Moses also stretched his hand over the waters and parted them. Who divided the water? We know God did; Moses can't divide a sea. But God said, "As for you, Moses, . . . stretch out *your hand* over the sea *and divide it.*" God told *Moses* to divide the water.

How can Moses perform such a feat?

Moses could divide the Sea because God was *with him*—just as He promised at the burning bush. Indeed, through covenant, as Moses stood before the people beside the sea, as he surrendered, he was *one with* God. God was *one with* him.

New Covenant Application

We will not go through the same course Moses did. However, we will have obstacles in our lives that seem impossible, hurdles that we cannot handle on our own—challenges devised to turn our focus from the problem to God so that we can hope and trust in Him. It is through such tests we learn that indeed, God is with us. In covenant, He has committed to be with us in all of His power and might.

However, if we look at the approaching "chariots," we will miss His salvation. We will become wrapped in fear, wringing our hands and blaming those around us. If we want to experience God's salvation, we need to stand still and look expectantly to Him.

The God that protected Israel is the same yesterday, today, and forever.[20] He is God of all who yield their life to Him through Jesus Christ. We can trust in Him.

The challenge for us is to stand still, expectant to see God work. When He fights for us, the battle is won. Really won.

Faith and salvation come as we gaze at our covenant God, remembering His promises to His children. Indeed, He will be with us wherever we go.

Moses knew God was with him, but Israel still had many lessons ahead.

Chapter 5 Questions for Reflection and Discussion

1. Read Exodus 3:10–12.
    - What sign did God promise Moses?
    - Why would this stretch Moses' faith?
    - Have you felt that God was asking something similar of you?
    - Did the Lord meet your needs to build your faith like He did Moses?

2. Why did Moses resist God's call to lead His children to freedom?

3. How did God meet Moses where He was and move Him to a place of faith?

4. Israel saw the signs and wonders that Moses saw, so they, too, knew God was powerful. When they were trapped in the pass with the army approaching behind them (Ex. 14), what had Moses learned that Israel did not know yet?

5. Read Matthew 28:19–20, Hebrews 7:25, 13:5–6.
    - When you face hard times, do you know that the Lord is with you?
    - How has He met you where you are to help you learn that truth?
    - If you sometimes think, "I know God does 'that' for others, but why would He do it for me?" how can you turn the thought to faith that God is with you too?

Chapter 6

God Proves Faithful to His People

When God cut the covenant with Abraham, He promised to be in covenant with Abraham's descendants and to provide all their needs too. We have seen how many of those descendants turned from God and no longer walked in covenant. By the time the Moses returned to Egypt, it might seem that the covenant was no longer in effect. However, the Word of the Lord does not fail. God is true to His promises even when we do not understand His ways. He had told Abraham,

> I will establish My covenant between Me and you and your descendants after you throughout their generations for an everlasting covenant, to be God to you and to your descendants after you. And I will give to you and to your descendants after you, the land of your sojournings, all the land of Canaan, for an everlasting possession; and I will be their God. (Gen. 17:7–8)

Jacob's descendents did not experience fulfillment of these promises. They were enslaved in Egypt, not living in Canaan. The cruelty and deprivation they experienced did not feel like protection and provision. Many may not have even realized that their father Abraham was in a blood covenant relationship with the living God, much less that He was their God.

Israel had been in bondage for generations. They didn't know what it meant to be covenant people. Slavery tampers with the soul of those caught in it. Slaves tend to lose initiative and their sense of self-worth. They begin to see themselves as possessions, as nobodies, without freedom of choice. It would seem like a fairy tale to a nation of slaves to hear that God was their provision, that all He had was at their disposal. After four hundred years, how could their imaginations stretch to encompass such thoughts?

Before they could enjoy the blessings that were rightfully theirs, Israel's way of thinking needed to be transformed. They needed to be trained to think and act as covenant people. God's call to Moses involved more than freeing Israel from slavery. Moving out of spiritual bondage and into renewed faith and relationship with their God was probably more significant than the move back to the land that was promised to them.

God Reveals Himself to His People

First, Israel needed to know their God. Immediately after Moses' arrival in Egypt, the Lord began to reveal Himself to His people. As God had instructed, Moses and Aaron gathered the elders of Israel, spoke the words of the Lord, and performed signs that showed His power.[1] When the men of Israel "heard that the LORD was concerned about the sons of Israel and that He had seen their affliction, then they bowed low and worshiped" (Ex. 4:29–31).

News of the Lord's concern must have filled their hearts with hope. For the first time in generations—even centuries—God spoke to them. He cared. In response, the Israelites spontaneously bowed low and worshipped the God who would free them.

Israel's hope, however, was quickly dashed. Pharaoh did not grant their appeal to go worship as a nation. Instead, he made their conditions harsher. The taskmasters increased the slaves burden by making them gather their own straw to make bricks, while telling them, "'Complete your work quota, your daily amount, just as when you had straw." The slaves who were foremen over them were beaten and asked, "Why have you not completed your required amount either yesterday or today in making brick as previously?" (Ex. 5:6–7, 13–14).

Their faith was shaken as their hope of freedom led to further oppression. Israel's foremen appealed to Pharaoh. However, in response they experienced even harsher treatment. They then cried out to Moses and Aaron: "May the LORD look upon you and judge you, for you have made us odious in Pharaoh's sight and in the sight of his servants, to put a sword in their hand to kill us" (Ex. 5:21).

Moses didn't understand what was going on. He went to the Lord asking, Why do You hurt Your people? Why did You send me if it would lead to further suffering rather than to freedom?[2] The Lord reassured Moses, "Now you shall see what I will do to Pharaoh; for under compulsion *he shall let them go*, and under compulsion *he shall drive them out of his land.*" (Ex. 6:1–5, emphasis added).

Once again, God confirmed the covenant originally cut with Abraham. He assured Moses that Israel would be freed, revealed His name, JHWH* (Jehovah, Jahweh, or LORD), which means self-existent, or eternal.[3] Through His name, He assured Moses once again that He was the "I AM" and would be with them.[4]

*The English translation for JHWH is often "the Lord," when in fact it is a name (JHWH, Jahweh, or Jehovah), not a title. God said, "I appeared to Abraham, Isaac, and Jacob, as God Almighty, but ***by*** My name, LORD, ***I did not make Myself known to them***" (Ex. 6:3).

But He didn't stop there. God continued reassuring Moses with covenant language, telling Him to tell Israel, "I am the LORD, and *I will bring you out*, . . . and *I will deliver you.*" He told them that He would redeem them, and that they would be His people and He would be their God. In closing, He said, "'and you shall know that *I am the LORD your God*, who brought you out from under the burdens of the Egyptians. And *I will bring you to the land* which I swore to give to Abraham, Isaac, and Jacob, and *I will give it to you for a possession*; I am the LORD" (Ex. 6:6–8, emphasis added).

Those were mighty big promises for slaves who had never known the power of God. He may have been the God of Abraham, but what did it mean that He would be their God too? How could He free them from slavery? Furthermore, the distant, Promised Land was beyond their experience and hope. Before the Israelites could accept such promises with sustained hope, they needed to know their God was powerful enough to fulfill His Word. To Israel, their bondage was a greater reality than the promises of their God.

"So Moses spoke thus to the sons of Israel, but they did not listen to Moses on account of their despondency and cruel bondage" (Ex. 6:9).

God's Hidden Agenda

Moses came to free his people, but God had other purposes in mind. If all He wanted was to liberate His children, He could have changed Pharaoh's heart immediately. Instead, Pharaoh kept hardening his heart through a series of devastating plagues.[5] Finally, during the sixth plague, the Bible says that, "the LORD hardened Pharaoh's heart" (Ex. 9:12, emphasis added).

God prevented the release of Israel. He would not do that without a purpose. What could be God's motive for prolonging Israel's suffering? What could they gain from constant cruelty?

During the delay, God demonstrated His power and might. He ravaged Egypt with frogs, gnats, flies, disease, boils, locusts, and more—all under the watchful eye of Israel. Israel needed to witness God's power, protection and provision before they entered the wilderness. Through the plagues, they had a close-up demonstration. They witnessed miraculous wonders at the hand of *their* God, for the purpose of *their* release.

Egypt also saw that the God of Israel was superior to Egyptian gods. God's reputation as the supreme God spread to other nations, too. That proved beneficial as Israel faced hostile nations in coming years. Before the plague of hail, the Lord told Moses to tell Pharaoh, "For this time I will send all My plagues . . . *so that you may know that there is no one like Me in all the earth*. . . . Indeed, for this cause I have allowed you to remain, *in order to show you My power, and in order to proclaim My name through all the earth*" (Ex. 9:14–16, emphasis added).

For the tenth and final plague, the Lord commanded each household to take a perfect lamb, kill it at twilight, put the blood on the doorposts in a prescribed manner, and eat the whole lamb as part of a Passover Meal. That night, the death angel passed through the streets of Egypt. Where blood was not sprinkled on the doorposts of the homes, all the first-born of man and beasts died. Weeping and wailing filled the land.

However, God told His children:

> The blood shall be a sign for you on the houses where you live; and when I see the blood I will pass over you, and no plague will befall you to destroy you. . . . Now this day will be a memorial to you, and you shall celebrate it as a feast to the LORD; throughout your generations you are to celebrate it. (Ex. 12:13–14)

Through the blood, the children of Israel declared their allegiance to God, and were saved from the death angel and from slavery. All these events took place because, "God heard their groaning; and *God remembered His covenant with Abraham*, Isaac, and Jacob" (Ex. 2:24, emphasis added).

Establishing Covenant with Israel

God did more than remember the covenant with Abraham. He sought to teach Abraham's children about the covenant and to build a relationship with them. He also confirmed each covenant exchange. God made sure His people understood His commitment to them by fulfilling—and sometimes repeating—the covenant exchanges with the nation.

In this chapter we will look at the cutting of the flesh; the exchange of names; the promise of protection (weapon exchange); and the promise of provision (coat exchange) as the covenant was confirmed with the nation of Israel. In the next chapter, we will discuss the covenant meal, the blessings and curses, and the memorials.

Cutting the Flesh

As discussed earlier, the letting of blood distinguishes a blood covenant from all others and marks the person as one who is in covenant. Cutting the flesh is the personal, active, and visible step of commitment. In obedience to God's command to Abraham, circumcision had continued while the Israelites were in slavery. God's directive to Moses to circumcise his son as he traveled from Midian to Egypt[6] is further confirmation of the continued importance of circumcision for those in covenant.

We also see its importance in God's dealings with the nation of Israel. Only men who were circumcised were allowed to join in the Passover Meal.* It was a prerequisite for obtaining freedom from slavery and for the promised protection and provision. All who left Egypt with Moses had been circumcised.[7]

*Exodus 12:43–49. Gentiles who celebrated Passover and left Egypt with Israel were all circumcised in order to be received as part of the covenant family of God. Gentiles always had the opportunity to become part of the covenant, but they had to first be circumcised.

The Lord also commanded Joshua to circumcise all the sons of Israel immediately after crossing the Jordan River into the promised land of Canaan, "for all the people who came out were circumcised, but all the people who were born in the wilderness along the way as they came out of Egypt had not been circumcised" (Josh. 5:5). They could not move into the provision God had for them without the sign of covenant.

As with Abraham, the covenant mark was hidden, requiring them to walk by faith. The only way others would know of their relationship with a covenant God was if, and when, He made His presence known.

Name Exchange

The exchange of names is also evident with the nation of Israel. While in the wilderness, the Israelites were constantly called "the children of God," or "the people of God." In Exodus alone, the Lord used the intimate possessive pronoun nineteen times to refer to the Israelites as "My people."[8] Ownership implied by use of the possessive is appropriate only for a blood covenant. No other people were spoken of so intimately. The Lord is also referred to as the "God of Israel" 202 times in the Old Testament. Whenever these terms are used, they highlight the covenant relationship Israel had with the living God.**

**Other tribes also came to know the Israelites and to fear them because of the name of God and the power associated with His name. They were known as the people whose God would fight for them and were greatly feared in the region because of the power of their God.

> "Then they will know that *I, the LORD their God*, am with them, and that they, the house of Israel, *are My people*," declares the Lord God. "As for you, *My sheep*, the sheep of My pasture, you are men, and *I am your God*," declares the Lord GOD. (Ezek. 34:30–31, emphasis added)

The name of God is also carried in Israel's name. While there is no record of a ceremonial exchange of names, there was an intentional, significant change initiated by God. The nation was called Israel after their father, Israel, who had brought them to Egypt. As we have said, God changed his name from Jacob, *deceiver*, to Israel as he returned to the Promised Land.[9] The Lord said, "Your name shall no longer be Jacob, but Israel; for you have striven with God and with men and have prevailed" (Gen. 32:28).

The first part of Israel, Isra, means *to rule* or *have power*, indicating God's intention for His people to rule with Him. *El* meaning *might* or *power,* is the name used for the Almighty God.* When the Lord changed Jacob's name to Isra**el,** (Isra-*el*), He inserted His name, **El**, thus completing the exchange of names between God and Israel.

**Strong's*, H3478. *Yisra'el*, from H8280. sarah, saw-raw'; a prim. root; to prevail:--have power (as a prince), and H410. 'el, ale; short. from H352; "strength; as adj. mighty; espec. the Almighty (but used also of any deity):--God."

Weapon Exchange

God was also a shield to His children, protecting them and their cattle from the plagues of Egypt.[10] Time after time, disaster fell on the Egyptians, but the Israelites were spared. God was their shield. As they fled Egypt, God—as a cloud—shielded them from the pursuing Egyptian army while they crossed the Red Sea. He then released the waters and drowned the enemy army.[11] Egypt was destroyed and has never regained status as the most powerful nation of the world.

In addition, while they were in the wilderness, even though they had been slaves and were not trained in battle, God protected Israel during confrontations with hostile nations. Significantly, they did not win through cunning military prowess, but through unconventional warfare. They were dependent on God for victory.

For example, when fighting Amalek at Rephidim, Moses' hands had to be lifted to the Lord throughout the battle. Every time he dropped his hands, the enemy prevailed.[12] Later, at Jericho they won by walking around the city. Then when they shouted and blew trumpets, the city walls fell.[13] God demonstrated that *He* would fight for them. They did not need any other protection.

However, at times, Israel did not experience God's sovereign protection—because they willfully broke the covenant, thus earning the penalty of death. The best-known example was when they made a molten calf in the wilderness and worshiped it. The Lord did not even claim them as His children when speaking to Moses about it.

> "Go down at once, for your people, whom you brought up from the land of Egypt, have corrupted themselves. *They have quickly turned aside from the way which I commanded them.* They have made for themselves a molten calf, and have worshiped it, and have sacrificed to it, and said, 'This is your god, O Israel, who brought you up from the land of Egypt!'" (Ex. 32:7–8, emphasis added)

The nation of Israel rejected God for an idol. They even credited the molten calf with their delivery from slavery. In return, "the LORD said to Moses, 'I have seen this people, and behold, they are an obstinate people. Now then let Me alone, that My anger may burn against them, and that I may destroy them; and I will make of you a great nation'" (Ex. 32:9–10).

Moses interceded on behalf of Israel, reminding God of what other nations would say and of what He had promised to Abraham, Isaac, and Jacob. "So the LORD changed His mind about the harm which He said He would do to His people" (Ex. 32:14).* Rather than being protected, without Moses' intercession, they would have perished under the wrath of God, and justifiably so according to the terms of covenant. God's mercy, and faithfulness—with Moses' intercession—prevented the Lord from wiping out the nation and rebuilding the covenant line from a remnant.**

*The covenant was everlasting because God would remain faithful to it. However, as the people were unfaithful, they were deserving of death. If the covenant had continued through Moses and it would still have been an everlasting covenant.

**See Deuteronomy 9:5, 29. The covenant is everlasting, but it carries curses as well as blessings. God often blesses when it is not warranted. However, when the terms of the covenant are broken, curses are the deserved consequence. God is a jealous God as well as a God of love and mercy. There is reason to fear Him if we do not seek to follow and obey.

Covenant Provision

The Lord also provided for His people. When speaking to Abraham about the period of slavery to come, the Lord declared, "Afterwards [Abraham's descendants] will come out with many possessions" (Gen. 15:14). Hundreds of years later, He was faithful to fulfill His Word. "Now the sons of Israel . . . requested from the Egyptians articles of silver and articles of gold, and clothing; and the LORD had given the people favor in the sight of the Egyptians, so that they let them have their request. Thus they plundered the Egyptians" (Ex. 12:35–36).

The people of Egypt were eager to get rid of the Israelites, whatever the cost. They piled treasures on their slaves as they sent them away. In one night, Egypt was stripped of riches, making Israel a wealthy nation.[14]

The Lord also provided their simple daily needs in the wilderness. In spite of forty years of wandering in harsh desert conditions, the Israelites' shoes and clothing did not wear out.[15] In addition, a cloud provided a climate-controlled environment protecting them from the heat of the sun in the daytime and offering light and warmth by night.[16] God provided all their needs. However, some of the provisions were also a source of testing.

Proving through Provision

In spite of God's miraculous deliverance and provision while freeing them, the Israelites did not recognize the Lord as their provider. For example, after three days in the desert, Israel was without water. They feared they would die of thirst and immediately blamed Moses for their lack. Was it Moses' fault? God led them to the desert. Moses could not provide water.

Nevertheless, Moses could look to the God of Israel. Supplying drink for millions of people in the midst of a vast desert was no problem for the Creator of all water. Neither was their lack of water an oversight on His part.

It was a test. Exodus 15:25 tells us, "There [God] made for them a statute and regulation, and *there He tested [proved] them*" (emphasis added).

After the people grumbled at Moses, "What shall we drink?" Moses cried out to the Lord, and the Lord showed him a tree. When he threw it in the water, the water became sweet.

Then Moses said, "*If* you will give earnest heed to the voice of the LORD your God, and do what is right in His sight, and give ear to His commandments, and keep all His statutes, *[then]* I will put none of the diseases on you which I have put on the Egyptians; for I, the LORD, am your healer" (Ex. 15:26).

The recent slaves had not learned yet that God would provide for them. If the Lord met all their needs before the people were aware of them, they would never recognize where the provision came from. Need for water presented a teachable moment. It was a test to teach them to cry out to God when they had a need. In addition, the Lord gave instruction about heeding His voice and promised them blessings if they listened and followed Him.

As slaves, they had always looked to the Egyptians for their provision. Instead of looking to man, they needed to depend on God to meet their needs. If they would heed His voice and obey His statutes, God promised they would be cared for.

One step at a time, the Lord demonstrated that He was their God, their provision. He sent deliverers to lead them out of Egypt, loaded them down with wealth, guided and protected them with a cloud, and instructed them through miraculous provision of water, as well as promising future blessings. God gave the children of Israel abundant evidence of His faithfulness to provide, but they had not yet learned to look to Him when in need—even for water.

Israel Tests God

Before long, the people found themselves without water a second time. However, instead of seeking God, they once again "quarreled with Moses and said, 'Give us water that we may drink.'"

> And Moses said to them, "Why do you quarrel with me? *Why do you test the LORD*?"
>
> But the people thirsted there for water; *and they grumbled against Moses* and said, "Why, now, have you brought us up from Egypt, to kill us and our children and our livestock with thirst?" (Ex. 17:2–3, emphasis added)

God had previously proven He would provide water. Yet, when given another opportunity to trust Him for drink, they looked to Moses as their provision, grumbling and blaming *him* for their problems. They switched their dependence from Egypt to Moses, not God. Even after being reprimanded, "Why do you test the Lord?" they continued to grumble at Moses. Water was a tool to point to the real issue—their lack of dependence on God and trusting in Him.

Robert: In the 1970s, we suffered a reversal in finances and considered Kay getting a job. However, after prayer, we felt she needed to stay home with our two small children. When I began seminary, further reducing our income, we continued to feel that Kay needed to stay home. God gave us confidence that He would provide for our needs.

And He did, sometimes dramatically. Two years later, we learned of the blood covenant and understood that God had committed Himself through covenant to provide for us.

Seeing the Lord provide through unconventional means became an exciting adventure. When I became a pastor, we feared that with a salary we would again look to man as our provider. For us, like with Israel, learning to trust God, not man, with daily needs takes time and is a constant challenge.

Israel's bad attitude and lack of faith was recorded for future generations to see. "And he named the place Massah [test] and Meribah [quarrel] because of the quarrel of the sons of Israel, and because they tested God, saying, 'Is the LORD among us, or not?'" (Ex. 17:7). In spite of their slowness to learn, the Lord was faithful to provide for Israel by causing water to come from a rock.

It is easy to rationalize when faith is lacking. The children of Israel could have made excuses. They could have said they didn't have an example of faith to follow, or that everybody *knows* the desert doesn't have water for two million people.

But God didn't make—or allow—excuses for them. He asked, "Why do you test Me? Why do you not trust Me when I have proven Myself to you?"

The children of Israel had still not learned their lesson. Consequently, God gave them more opportunities to learn the truth that He was their provision. He used basic things in life to teach them, such as hunger. When they became hungry, rather than crying out to God, they once again grumbled at Moses. The "whole congregation" said, "'would that we had died by the LORD's hand in the land of Egypt, when we sat by the pots of meat, when we ate bread to the full; for you have brought us out into this wilderness to kill this whole assembly with hunger'" (Ex. 16:3).

They failed to remember what God had done on their behalf. In fact, their despair from lack of food was so strong they would rather have died in slavery. Once again, they saw Moses as their source and blamed him for bringing them into the wilderness. Their faith didn't grow because they continued looking to man rather than looking to God.

In spite of their lack of trust, God said, "I will rain *bread from heaven* for you" (Ex. 16:4). He gave them the perfect food, containing everything they needed. In response, they kept saying, "What is this?" ("Manna?") For forty years, they called God's bread from heaven, "manna." With ungrateful hearts, they kept on asking, "What is it?" Yet, amazingly their covenant partner kept providing for all their needs.[17]

Application: Parents can identify with what it's like to give children something in answer to their request and encounter a response of ungratefulness. Even if the gift is costly and is good for them, if it isn't what is expected, sometimes the response rings with "what is this?" At times, it seems that no matter what parents do, children always want something else.

Even as adults, when our expectations are not met, it seems it is easier to grumble than be grateful. Like Israel, we too often focus on what we don't have, rather than on God's faithfulness and our blessings. Is it any wonder that God calls us children?

Israel was never satisfied with the bread from heaven. They cried and said, "'Who will give us meat to eat? We remember the fish which we used to eat free in Egypt, the cucumbers and the melons and the leeks and the onions and the garlic, but now our appetite is gone. There is nothing at all to look at except this manna'" (Num. 11:4–6).

The Lord was not pleased with the ungratefulness of His greedy children, but it didn't change His graciousness towards them. He told Moses to tell the people to consecrate themselves because they would have meat to eat the next day. God said, "'You shall eat, not one day, nor two days, nor five days . . . , but a whole month, until it comes out of your nostrils and becomes loathsome to you; *because you have rejected the LORD who is among you* and have wept before Him, saying, 'Why did we ever leave Egypt?'" (Num. 11:18–20).

God was their provision. He provided the quail they wanted, even though they murmured among themselves[18] instead of asking Him.

In contrast, by their continued dependence on Moses and ungratefulness for what God did, Israel rejected God, even after He had freed them from bondage. Their lack of trust was more than a lack of faith. By not acknowledging God, they:

· failed to recognize what He had done in the past;
· rejected His love and care;
· denied His power;
· denied His desire to provide;
· doubted that He knew what was best for them; and
· questioned whether He desired the best for them.

Lack of faith in God is a denial of Who He is. It is rejection and rebellion.

Israel did not lack nutrition. They did not need meat. Neither did they deserve a special treat. They were ungrateful for His faithful provision, and murmured rather than asking politely. They were even wishing they were back in slavery. Why would the Lord overlook their ungratefulness, rejection, and rebellion?

He did it because He had cut a covenant with their father, Abraham, and He had confirmed the covenant with them. The Lord was faithful to the covenant.

However, He was grieved. He desired an intimate relationship with Israel. In contrast, they wanted only to fulfill the desires of the flesh. The Lord granted their request, but with it they received leanness for their souls.[19]

New Covenant Application

Our God is the same yesterday, today, and forever.[20] His desire for intimacy has not changed. He created man in His image and enjoyed fellowship with him in the garden. After that relationship was broken by sin, He chose Abraham to cut a covenant and reestablish intimate fellowship. When the time was right, He came to Moses to renew that relationship, but His people could not—or would not—see it. They continued to reject Him and to test Him.

In the fullness of time, He sent His Son to establish a new and better covenant, one that has greater provision for intimacy. But do His people see it today? Do we look to God or to man to meet our needs? Do we desire the intimacy with Him made possible through His Son? Or do we too seek to fulfill the desires of the flesh?

The almighty, living, covenant-making God has not changed. He continues to be faithful and to seek fellowship. He is looking for those who desire intimate friendship with Him.[21]

Chapter 6 Questions for Reflection and Discussion

1. Read Exodus 32:11–14. God was ready to destroy all of His chosen people and create a new nation through Moses. Based on what you've learned about covenant, why did God have the right to be angry?
   - How does Moses' appeal show an intimate understanding of covenant?
   - What false gods are worshiped today that could incur severe consequences? Why?

2. Read 1 Peter 4:10–14, Read James 1:2–4, 12. The Lord tested Israel through the need for water and their desire for different food. We, too, are tested—by things beyond our control and by fleshly desires.
   - How is your faith being tested?
   - How are you responding?

     Self effort? Looking to man? or Looking to God?

     With fear and murmuring, or with faith?

3. In what ways has God shown Himself faithful to you?
   - In protection
   - In provision

Chapter 7

The Cost of Unbelief

What would it take for Israel to learn to trust God for protection and provision? As a loving Father, the Lord was with them every step of their journey, guiding, protecting, and providing all their needs. All they needed to do was rely on Him. However, Israel was slow to acknowledge God, much less trust Him.

As in all blood covenants, God established memorials to remind His people of the covenant. In addition, He provided opportunities to teach future generations about Himself and the commitment He had made to them. The Lord established seven reminders to keep the covenant before them at all times.

Seven Memorials

The Hebrew verb for "memorial" (*zeker*) can also be translated "remembrance." The word is used over three hundred times in the Old Testament. The Lord repeatedly told His people to remember, and He established specific reminders to help them.[1]

1. His Name

When God told Moses that He was "I AM," Jehovah, He declared His name to be a memorial, saying, "Thus shalt thou say unto the children of Israel, the LORD God of your fathers, the God of Abraham, the God of Isaac, and the God of Jacob, hath sent me unto you: this is my name forever, and *this is my memorial unto all generations*" (Exod. 3:15, emphasis added).

God is called by many names in Scripture. For example, after the battle with Amalek, the Lord also commanded that His name, Jehovah Nissi (The Lord is My Banner) be a memorial.[2] Each name identifies and memorializes a different quality of His nature. We can know Him more fully by studying His names.[3]

2. Stone Memorials

As the children of Israel entered the Promised Land, Joshua built an altar as a memorial and said, "*Let this be a sign among you* . . . because the waters of the Jordan were cut off before the ark of the covenant of the LORD; . . . . So *these stones shall become a memorial* to the sons of Israel forever" (Josh. 4:4–7, emphasis added).

In addition, memorials were built with uncut stones at Mount Gerizim and Mount Ebal. The law was written on them so the people would never forget the law and the pageant of blessings and the curses.[4] The stone memorials were permanent, visible reminders to clarify and strengthen Israel's relationship with the Lord.

3. The Sabbath

> So the sons of Israel shall observe the sabbath, to celebrate the sabbath throughout their generations *as a perpetual covenant*. It is *a sign* between Me and the sons of Israel forever; for in six days the LORD made heaven and earth, but on the seventh day He ceased from labor, and was refreshed. (Exod. 31:13–17, emphasis added)[5]

Israel was an agricultural society. Their work did not stop at the end of six days. It took faith and commitment to set aside personal needs for a whole day out of each week. Through honoring the Lord for one day out of seven, Israel acknowledged God as their exceedingly great reward. God blessed them as a people when they honored that seventh day of rest.

Every seventh year, they were also to let their land lie fallow, not planting anything. During that year, they could eat from the abundance of the last six years and of anything that came up voluntarily.[6] On the seventh set of the seven years, the Year of Jubilee, they were to celebrate a whole year. That year, they were to free all Israelite slaves and return land to its original Hebrew family—all in faith and obedience to God as a memorial of His faithfulness to them.

Israel became diligent, even legalistic, about taking a Sabbath rest, but there is no record in Scripture indicating that they faithfully observed the Year of Jubilee. Whether because they didn't take God's command seriously, were rebellious, or lacked faith, Israel was not as obedient in celebrating Jubilee. But God was serious, and Israel's lack of obedience led to consequences. They were made captives of Babylon to fulfill His command. They remained servants "*to fulfill the word of the LORD* by the mouth of Jeremiah, *until the land had enjoyed its sabbaths*. All the days of its desolation it kept Sabbath until seventy years were complete" (2 Chron. 36:20–21, emphasis added).

4. The Promised Land

God gave the land to Abraham and his covenant descendants as their inheritance from the Lord. It was apportioned to the tribes and divided among the families.[7] Land was to stay in the family to which it was allotted. If it was sold because of financial need, it was to return to the family every Year of Jubilee (forty-ninth year). It was a permanent possession of the original families, given by God and protected by His commands. Though *zakar* is not used in relation to the land, its permanent possession by the designated families served as a reminder that the Lord was their covenant provider.

5. The Tabernacle

> And you shall take the atonement money from the sons of Israel, and shall give it for the service of the tent of meeting, *that it may be a memorial* for the sons of Israel before the LORD. (Exod. 30:16, emphasis added)

The Lord directed Moses to take a census of the people. Every male twenty years old and over was to give a ransom for himself to be used for the service of the tabernacle.[8] The tabernacle was God's residence in their midst. It led the way and was the focal point as they wandered in the wilderness. Their ransom to God for the tabernacle recognized and honored God. The tabernacle was a constant reminder, a memorial to God.

6. The Feasts

The Passover Meal was instituted as a memorial to be celebrated annually on the anniversary of the Passover in Egypt. "Now this day will be a *memorial* to you, and you shall celebrate it as a feast to the LORD; throughout your generations you are to celebrate it as a *permanent ordinance*" (Ex. 12:14, emphasis added).

During their first year in the wilderness, God instituted six other annual feasts to be celebrated throughout the year. They emphasized concepts such as sacrifices, covering by blood, provision, and redemption. Each fulfilled a different purpose in reminding His children about different aspects of Himself and the relationship He desired with them.[9]

7. Tithe

> And to the sons of Levi, behold, I have given all the tithe in Israel for an inheritance, in return for their service which they perform . . . . Only the Levites shall perform the service of the tent of meeting . . . *it shall be a perpetual statute* throughout your generations, and among the sons of Israel they shall have no inheritance. (Num. 18:21, 23, emphasis added)[10]

Giving a tenth of all increase back to God requires faith that God's provision will continue to be adequate. It is a constant reminder that God is their source. It is also a test—a proving—that reflects how much faith and belief God's children have that He is their provider.

One memorial was not enough. Israel needed constant reminders of their God. Seven memorials gave continuous prompts for Israel to remember the faithfulness of their God. The number seven is also closely related to the word "oath" in Hebrew. Having seven memorials is significant, placing emphasis on the oath of covenant that God made to His children and of His faithfulness to it.

Covenant Meal

Through several steps, the Lord renewed the covenant with the nation of Israel, thus clearly defining His relationship with His chosen people as a covenant relationship. First, He gave the Ten Commandments in Exodus 20 to outline rules of relationship. He then gave laws that interpret application of the Ten Commandments in specific detail. The Lord ended by telling them not to make covenants with the people in the land or with their gods.[11]

Then, as recorded in Exodus 24, the Lord called Moses, Aaron, Nadab, Abihu and seventy elders to come up on the mountain, but only Moses went near God. "Then Moses came and recounted to the people all the words of the LORD and all the ordinances; and all the people answered with one voice, and said, 'All the words which the LORD has spoken we will do!'" (Exod. 24:3).

Moses wrote down all the words given them while on the mountain. In the morning, he built an altar with twelve pillars for the twelve tribes—a significant representation of *all* the people—and offered sacrifices. "Then he took the *book of the covenant* and read it in the hearing of the people; and they said, 'All that the Lord has spoken we will do, and we will be obedient!'" (Exod. 24:7, emphasis added).

Moses took blood from the sacrifices, sprinkled it on the people, and said, "Behold *the blood of the covenant, which the* L*ORD* *has made [*karath, *cut] with you* in accordance with all these words" (Exod. 24:8, emphasis added).

Then, Moses, Aaron, Nadab, and Abihu, with seventy elders went up the mountain, "and *they saw the God of Israel*; and under His feet there appeared to be a pavement of sapphire, as clear as the sky itself . . . and they beheld God, and *they ate and drank*" (Exod. 24:4–11, emphasis added).

First, Moses read the terms of the covenant and the people agreed to them. He then sprinkled them with the blood of the covenant. Next, the almighty God invited the elders up on the mountain so they could enjoy a meal together. How much more intimate could you be with the living God? At God's initiation, invitation, and direction, in the presence of God they "ate and drank." In the midst of the ceremony reinforcing the covenant, it seems that they had a covenant meal together.

The word covenant is not mentioned in connection with the meal. However, this intimate meal, shared by God and Israel's leaders, has the appearance of a celebration of the blood covenant, a confirmation of the pact made with Abraham. In addition, it takes place within a setting of covenant renewal. The Lord took positive steps to establish covenant communion with His children.

Then He went a step further. The elders were new at walking in covenant. They needed help so they would know how to teach others how to live in covenant with the living God.

The Lord met them in their need. He told Moses, "'Come up to Me on the mountain and remain there, and I will give you the stone tablets with the law and the commandment which I have written for their instruction'" (Exod. 24:12). God gave them guidelines so they would not have any doubts as to live while in covenant relationship with Him.*

*Deuteronomy 4:10–14 further confirms that this was part of a covenant renewal.The remainder of the chapter reminds Israel of God's goodness to them and contains strong cautions and warnings to remain faithful to the covenant.

The Israelites Move Forward

After the elders of Israel celebrated the meal with God and received the Ten Commandments, the nation camped at the base of Mount Sinai. For a year, they brought order to the new nation, built the tabernacle, learned the statutes of the Lord, and consecrated the Levites. One year after their deliverance, on the first day of the first month, they set up the tabernacle for the first time. The cloud covered it and the glory of the Lord filled it. Nobody could go near.[12]

On the fourteenth day of the second month, they marked the anniversary of their miraculous deliverance by celebrating Passover.[13] Imagine what it would be like to be part of the first tribute to their deliverance, celebrating with people who had experienced bondage, witnessed miracles, and tasted freedom for the first time—with God's miraculous acts fresh on their minds. What a celebration, reliving the mighty things God had done.

Six days later, on the twentieth day of the second month, the cloud lifted from over the tabernacle and began to move. With the tabernacle in their midst, demonstrating the presence of God, the children of Israel once again set out for the Promise Land.[14] After such clear reminders that God was with them, faith would surely be high and they would be full of expectation as they followed the cloud into the land of milk and honey.

But as God's Word tells us, it did not happen as we would expect. Numbers 10 tells of Israel's departure from Mount Sinai. Chapter 11 is filled with murmuring and complaints. Chapter 12 tells of the rebellion of Miriam and Aaron. In chapter 13, they approach their destination. The account begins with God telling Moses to send spies into "the land of Canaan, *which I am going to give to the sons of Israel*; you shall send a man from each of their fathers' tribes" (Num. 13:1, emphasis added).

If faith was not already high, it seems God's promise of land "which I am going to give to the sons of Israel," would ensure an unshakable confidence that God would work on their behalf, even as He had in Egypt, at the Red Sea, and against Amalek. All they had to do was obey, then watch and see what God would do.

However, at the end of forty days, when the spies returned, they had a mixed report. They agreed that it was a rich land, flowing with milk and honey, but they added, "Nevertheless, the people who live in the land are strong, and the cities are fortified and very large" (Num. 13:28).

The crowd reacted to the news. Caleb quieted them, then spoke words of faith to Moses, "We should by all means go up and take possession of it, for we shall surely overcome it" (Num. 13:30).

Ten of the spies, however, had a different perspective. They said, "We are not able to go up against the people, for they are too strong for us. . . . All the people whom we saw in it are men of great size. . . . We became like grasshoppers in our own sight, and so we were in their sight" (Num. 13:31–33).

The congregation listened to the voices of doubt, rather than the voice of faith. They wept and grumbled against Moses and Aaron, saying, "Would that we had died in the land of Egypt! Or that we had died in the wilderness!" (Num. 14:1–2). Instead of being full of faith, they were ready to appoint a leader and return to Egypt and slavery.

Moses and Aaron fell on their faces in front of the assembly. Joshua and Caleb tore their clothes in anguish. They sought to build faith in the congregation, saying,

> The land which we passed through to spy out is an exceedingly good land. If the Lord is pleased with us, then He will bring us into this land, and give it to us—a land which flows with milk and honey. Only do not rebel against the Lord; and do not fear the people of the land, for they shall be our prey. Their protection has been removed from them, and the Lord is with us; do not fear them. (Num. 14:7b–9)

Joshua and Caleb spoke with faith. God had chosen Israel. He promised them land as well as His presence with them. They were miraculously freed from slavery so they could possess it. To not follow Him was defiance. To *not* move forward was rebellion. Joshua and Caleb reflected the heart of God in their report.

The other spies reported, "We became like grasshoppers in our own sight." They missed God and lacked faith because they focused on themselves and looked with their natural eyes. The nation joined them, expressing their unbelief though murmuring and complaining.

In contrast, Joshua and Caleb looked at Israel's covenant God, and viewed the challenge through His eyes. They knew the outcome had nothing to do with them. They saw the giants, but Joshua and Caleb had faith that nothing could stand in the way of God.

Miraculous acts of God do not always lead to faith or to a close relationship with the Lord. The children of Israel had seen the power of God demonstrated more dramatically than anybody in history, but they did not enter the Promised Land because their faith was lacking.

They could have settled down in their own homes and feasted on fruit and vegetables, along with the meat, milk and honey they longed for. Instead, they wandered in the wilderness and ate "manna" for forty years. All because they did not trust God.

Nevertheless, the Lord continued to be faithful to His children. He met all their needs in the wilderness. Water flowed from rocks. Bread fell from heaven. Quail flew into camp. Shoes and clothing did not wear out. The cloud protected from the heat of day and the cold of night, offered guidance, and most importantly, gave assurance of God's presence with them.[15]

Nonetheless, the Israelites were not grateful for God's abundant provision; neither did they learn from it. They became accustomed to God's loving care and took the goodness of God for granted. In response, God said,

> How long will this people spurn Me? And how long will they not believe in Me, despite all the signs which I have performed in their midst?. . . How long shall I bear with this evil congregation who are grumbling against Me? I have heard the complaints of the sons of Israel.
>
> Surely you shall not come into the land in which I swore to settle you, except Caleb the son of Jephunneh and Joshua the son of Nun. (Num. 14:11, 27, 30)

Blessings and Curses

In spite of all God did, forty years later, when it was time to enter the Promised Land, the tribes were quick to forget the Lord as their covenant God. All who were over twenty when they came out of Egypt had died. A new generation now led Israel.

Consequently, anyone who had witnessed the miracles of the plagues and the dramatic escape across the Red Sea were children at the time. Very few had experienced the hardships of slavery. As leaders of their families, they had always had daily bread from heaven and shoes and clothing that did not wear out.

Furthermore, they grew up in a culture that had murmured and complained about God's faithful provision. The freed slaves still lacked faith. Many had died in the wilderness as a result of their disobedience. Scripture indicates that few Israelites developed faith or passed it on to their children when they died.

Therefore, before the new generation of Israelites settled the Promised Land in the name of their God, they needed to know that He was going with them. They also needed to understand the nature of their covenant relationship with Him.

So, the Lord orchestrated a dramatic ceremony to reenact the cutting of the covenant. If the whole nation participated in a covenant ceremony—rather than just the elders, as at Sinai—they should all gain first-hand understanding of the terms of covenant. Maybe this would lead them to turn to God, truly becoming one with Him.

After crossing the Jordan, at God's direction, the first thing Israel did was build an altar. They also built memorials, coated them with lime, and wrote the words of the law on them. However, the ceremony did not end with the law. After they crossed the Jordan, Moses charged the people, telling half the tribes to stand on Mount Gerizim and half to stand on Mount Ebal.[16]

They stood on Mount Gerizim and Mouth Ebal with the ark of the covenant and an altar between them. Oxen were sacrificed for burn offerings and peace offerings, with blood flowing down the valley.* With great pomp, Israel celebrated the covenant God had cut with Abraham.[17]

*The picture is reminiscent of covenant makers standing on each end of the figure eight speaking blessings and curses, with the split pieces of the animal lying in a pool of blood between them.

The ritual began with the Levites giving the twelve covenant charges recorded in Deuteronomy 27:15–26. After each one, the vast multitude responded with a loud "Amen." First was, "Cursed is the man who makes an idol or a molten image" and "cursed is he who dishonors his father or mother." The charges closed with, "cursed is he who does not confirm the words of this law by doing them."

For the complete charge, see Deuteronomy 27:9–26, or Appendix B.

After the charges, six tribes (more than a million people) stood on Mount Gerizim to bless the multitude on Mount Ebal. In most tribal covenants, a representative, such as a chief or warlord, would cut a covenant for the whole tribe. It is significant that God had all of the people participate in the blessings and curses.

> Now it shall be, *if* you will diligently obey the LORD your God, being careful to do all His commandments which I command you

today, the Lord your God will set you high above all the nations of the earth. And all these blessings shall come upon you and overtake you, *if* you will obey the LORD your God (v. 1, emphasis added).

Blessed shall be the offspring of your body and the produce of your ground and the offspring of your beasts, the increase of your herd . . . (v. 4).

The LORD will cause your enemies who rise up against you to be defeated before you; they shall . . . flee before you seven ways (v. 7).

The LORD will establish you as a holy people to Himself, as He swore to you, if you will keep the commandments of the LORD your God . . . All the peoples of the earth shall see that you are called by the name of the LORD; and they shall be afraid of you (vv. 9–10).

And the LORD will make you abound in prosperity, in the offspring of your body and in the offspring of your beast and in the produce of your ground . . . the land which the LORD swore to your fathers to give you (v. 11).

The LORD will open for you His good storehouse, the heavens, to give rain to your land in its season and to bless all the work of your hand; and you shall lend to many nations, but you shall not borrow (v. 12).

For the complete list of blessings, see Deuteronomy 28:1–14, or Appendix C.

The blessings were followed by a long declaration of curses proclaimed by the six tribes on Mount Ebal, including:

But it shall come about, if you will not obey the LORD your God, to observe to do all His commandments and His statutes . . . that all these curses shall come upon you and overtake you (v. 15).

Cursed shall be the offspring of your body and the produce of your ground, the increase of your herd . . . (v. 18).

The LORD will send upon you curses, confusion, and rebuke, in all you undertake to do, until you are destroyed and until you perish quickly, on account of the evil of your deeds, because you have forsaken Me (v. 20).

The LORD will smite you with madness and with blindness and with bewilderment of heart (v. 28).

> Your sons and your daughters shall be given to another people . . . but there shall be nothing you can do (v. 32).
>
> The alien who is among you shall rise above you higher and higher, but you shall go down lower and lower. He shall lend to you, but you shall not lend to him; he shall be the head, and you shall be the tail (vv. 43–44).
>
> So all these curses shall come on you and pursue you and overtake you until you are destroyed, *because you would not obey the LORD your God* by keeping His commandments and His statutes which He commanded you (v. 45, emphasis added).
>
> *Because you did not serve the LORD your God with joy and a glad heart,* . . . therefore you shall serve your enemies whom the LORD shall send against you, in hunger, in thirst, in nakedness, and in the lack of all things; and He will put an iron yoke on your neck until He has destroyed you (vv. 47–48 emphasis added).
>
> Then you shall eat the offspring of your own body . . . during the siege and the distress by which your enemy shall oppress you (v. 53).
>
> Moreover, the LORD will scatter you among all peoples, from one end of the earth to the other end of the earth; . . . And among those nations you shall find no rest . . . but there the LORD will give you a trembling heart, failing of eyes, and despair of soul. . . . So your life shall hang in doubt before you; and you shall be in dread night and day, and shall have no assurance of your life (vv. 64–66).

For a complete list of curses, see Deuteronomy 28:16–68 or Appendix D.

A multitude stood on each mountain, separated by a valley of sacrificial blood. Blessings and curses were read loud enough for all to hear. The children of God cried, "Amen" to each.

The scene would be unforgettable.

That is exactly what the Israelites needed. They needed to never forget that they were in covenant with the living God. They also needed to understand the blessings that were due them in covenant—and the curses should they be unfaithful.

Unlike tabernacle worship, where only men were allowed, at the covenant reenactment, the women and children participated. Everyone was included. It was important for each and every person to understand and to remember.

Why were the laws, blessings, and curses much more clearly stated with Israel than with Abraham when the covenant was first cut?

Could it be because God is a relational God? Through relationship, the Lord led Abraham step-by-step into a greater intimacy and deeper faith. It was not necessary to state the terms of the blessings and curses with Abraham because he responded to God. The Lord prefers a relationship built on love, not on a desire for blessing or fear of curses.

God demonstrated that love to Israel. He protected, provided for, and guided them. He also taught them—just as with Abraham. However, unlike Abraham, in return, they constantly tested Him. They murmured, complained, and disobeyed. They even went so far as to build an idol to take His place. They never developed an intimacy in which they followed God in love. With the Israelites, blessings and curses were needed.

Kay: When our youngest sons were two and three years old, I took them on their first trip to the mall. They entertained themselves by running under and around clothing racks and up and down the aisles. I was beside myself trying to shop while reining them in. Suddenly, I realized that I had not given them instructions. They didn't know how to behave. I stooped to their level, looked them in the eye and gave them guidelines to behave.

They were model children the rest of our time there. They needed guidelines. Likewise, Israel needed the law to know what God expected of them. He stooped to their level to instruct them.

The Lord desired a relationship with His people that didn't require Ten Commandments, laws, and a list of blessings and curses. He wanted an intimate relationship based on love, but His children were accustomed to external controls. Most of them never learned how to relate from the heart. Because of Israel's rebellion, God had no choice.

Before He gave the law and issued blessings and curses to inform them of the expectations of covenant, the Lord had told Israel, "And you shall love the Lord your God with all your heart and with all your soul and with all your might" (Deut. 6:5). His design and desire is to have a relationship with us based on love. Jesus later quoted His Father's words when asked which commandment was greatest.[18]

Jesus also said to love our neighbor as ourselves, and said, "On these two commandments depend the whole Law and the Prophets" (Matt. 22:39–40). The law is based on love. In His great mercy and love, the Lord saw that Israel lacked a clear understanding of what it meant to be in relationship with a covenant God. He met their need.*

*To distinguish between the Old Covenant and the New by saying the Old is a covenant of law, and the New is a covenant of love or grace is a misunderstanding. The penalty for breaking a covenant is death. If people are constantly bringing the death penalty on themselves—as Israel was—it is merciful to give them guidelines for how to live so they will know more clearly how to keep the covenant. The Ten Commandments (and following laws) were an expression of God's love, mercy, and grace to His children.

God Desires Intimacy with Us

God met us in our need, too. Three times, He has met us. First, He called a special people to Himself. He cut a covenant with Abraham, giving us a picture of the kind of relationship we have with Him and the nation made up of Abraham's offspring.

Second, when His total commitment through blood covenant was not enough to ensure a relationship of love and allegiance, God gave His children the Law, to help them understand how to live in righteous relationship with Him and with each other. However, even with wonderful blessings for those who keep the law, and terrible curses for those who broke it, God's children continued to break the law—and thus the covenant.

Third, God met us again. He sent Jesus Christ to take the curse for us, freeing us so we can be in relationship with the Almighty God. He has done everything to make an intimate relationship with Himself possible for us.

Through the history of Israel, we can see the cost of unbelief, but we do not have to follow in the path of Israel. God does not change. He is faithful. He doesn't force Himself on us, but His arms—and His heart—are open wide.

How we respond is up to us. We choose whether or not to acknowledge Him. We decide whether to trust—or murmur. We choose a relationship of intimacy and love—or one of legalism.

Jesus said, "Behold, I stand at the door and knock; if anyone hears My voice and opens the door, I will come in to him, and will dine with him, and he with Me" (Rev. 3:20).

Chapter 7 Questions for Reflection and Discussion

1. Just as Israel needed memorials, we need reminders to help us keep our focus on and our faith in God.
   - Which of the memorials which God established with Israel are significant in your life today?
   - What personal memorials serve as reminders for you?

2. In John, read chapters 14–17. Ask the Lord to reveal the nature of the relationship He desires with you. Listen to Jesus's heart. Make notes of what you hear concerning:
   - Covenant—of oneness?
   - Protection, and provision?
   - Desire for intimacy?
   - Desire for unity within His body?

3. In the story of Israel, we see how slow they were to learn that God wanted intimacy. What in your life indicates that your walk is one of love and intimacy or of law and legalism?

4. Jesus has not changed. You can be as close to Him as you want to be. What would it look like for you to experience intimate fellowship with the Lord? Share your desire with Him.

Chapter 8

David: A Covenant Man

David is a prime example in Scripture of a man who understood and walked in covenant faithfulness. He had a vital relationship with God and looked to Him when in need. Even as a shepherd boy, he was faithful to the Lord.

Many Psalms reveal David's confidence in God as his covenant provider. When he said, "We are His people and the sheep of His pasture" (Ps. 100:3b), he was painting a picture of covenant. Like sheep, we are dependent on our covenant Partner, our Shepherd, for everything, including food, water, protection, and health. Further confidence that his God would provide is evident in Psalm 23:1, "The Lord is *my* shepherd, *I shall not want*" (emphasis added).

The songs of worship that David sang while watching over the sheep give expression to his intimacy with the Lord. His music was so soothing that he was taken to the palace to play his harp to calm the troubled King Saul. Then a battle broke out and David had to go home.

Israel Under Siege

The Philistine army gathered in Judah at Socoh to face Israel. In response, Saul and his men camped in the valley of Elah to face the Philistines. Each of the armies stood on a mountain facing each other, with the valley between them.[1]

When challenged, Saul didn't have much choice but to assemble his men and prepare for battle against the mighty Philistines. However, although armies faced one another and combat seemed unavoidable, there was no fight.

Instead, Goliath, a giant who was over nine feet tall and wore a bronze helmet with armor weighing a hundred pounds, stepped forth from the Philistine army with his shield bearer before him. He shouted to Israel's army, taunting them to choose a man to come fight him. He said, "If he is able to fight with me and kill me, then we will become your servants; but if I prevail against him and kill him, then you shall become our servants and serve us" (1 Sam. 17:4–9).

He repeated his threat, "I defy the ranks of Israel this day; give me a man that we may fight together" (1 Sam. 17:10).

Goliath was confident. He asked for a man, any man willing to fight against him. But in all the army of Saul, no one would face the giant. Rather than meet the challenge, "when Saul and all of Israel heard those words of the Philistine, they were dismayed, and greatly afraid."[2]

Israel's warriors listened to Goliath and were distracted from God's truth by what their eyes saw (a nine-foot giant before them) and what their ears heard (daily taunts of defiance). They knew they had no chance against the towering giant. Was there a man who could stand up to Goliath?

No man was a match for the giant.

But what about their God? He promised to be a shield to them. Was Goliath a threat to Almighty God? Of course not—but God often waits for His covenant people to acknowledge Him before He acts.

The deception of the enemy led Israel to question themselves and their limited ability. They did not think to call on God when weak and afraid. They forgot that He is faithful to the covenant and He would be with them in their time of need.

Truth or Fact?

It's true that Saul's warriors were not strong enough to fight Goliath, right? Well, not exactly. It is fact. However, fact and truth are not always the same. According to the dictionary, a fact is something that is known to exist or something that actually happened.[3]

We can confirm facts with our senses. For example:

- Opposing armies encamped on opposing hills.
- For forty days, the giant Goliath taunted the army of Israel.
- David went to check on his brothers.
- Goliath was larger and stronger than anyone in Saul's army.

Those are facts. Each fact could also be considered true, because they are "in accordance with the actual state or conditions."[4]

The principle that David understood illustrates the deepest definition of Truth. Truth (with a capital T) is deeper than fact and broader than what is true. According to *Webster's College Dictionary*, truth is "an ideal or fundamental reality apart from and transcending perceived experience."[5] In other words, it is a reality that is beyond what our senses can perceive.

The Truth that God was David's protection is a reality that is greater than fact. It is a principle of life. However, even though Truth is bigger than experience, it can be experienced. When God gave David victory over a lion and a bear, he experienced the Truth that God was his protection.[6] He was able to defeat them because he was dependent on God, not on himself, for courage, strength, and for victory.

On the battlefield at Elah, the Truth was that they did not have to fight Goliath. They had a covenant God Who was one with them. He was their shield and protector. He would fight for them. The facts of Goliath's size and might (what is seen and heard) distracted the Israelites. They believed the fact, "We don't stand a chance"—which, in this case, was a lie that felt true—rather than believing the Truth that God would fight the battle for them.

Application: God is not the author of fear. When we are afraid, it is often because we are reacting to facts that our eyes see and our ears hear, rather than focusing on the truths of God's Word. We tend to equate fact with Truth when we look at lies through our physical eyes, rather than our spiritual eyes.

David Is Sent to the Battlefield

Back at David's home, we see that David's father—Jesse—was "advanced in years" and that he had eight sons. The three oldest, Eliab, Abinadab, and Shammah had gone to battle under Saul's command. Meanwhile, David, the youngest, tended his father's flock at Bethlehem.

The aging Jesse relied on his sons. With his three eldest in battle against a ruthless opponent, he would naturally be concerned and eager to hear from Eliab, Abinadab, and Shammah. However, for forty days, he didn't hear a word.

"Now Saul, and they, and all the men of Israel, were in the valley of Elah, fighting with the Philistines" (1 Sam. 17:19). Fighting *with* the Philistines? Well, they were *at war*. Their families at home thought they were fighting. However, it seems they were fighting fear in their hearts more than the Philistines. Every day on the battlefield when the giant came out, the army of Israel ran and hid like terrified children. The only news was "Israel is scared and runs and hides." Nobody wanted to report that. So, those at home waited.

Finally Jesse called David in from the fields and told him to take food to his brothers and bring back news of what was happening on the battlefield. Imagine the excitement of a young teenager upon learning that he could see the army fight a real battle. The night before he left, he probably dreamed of war all night, as boys would likely do. We know he awakened before dawn, left the sheep with a keeper, and left to take supplies to his brothers.

> He came to the circle of the camp while the army was going out in battle array shouting the war cry. And Israel and the Philistines drew up in battle array, army against army. Then David left his baggage in the care of the baggage keeper, and ran to the battle line and entered in order to greet his brothers. (1 Sam. 17:20–22)

David's excitement must have peaked as he finally reached the camp. He saw Israel's army moving to the mountaintop. He heard their war cry as they came together. He was probably wide-eyed as he rushed to greet his big brothers and catch a close-up view of the action.

While David was talking with his brothers, Goliath, the Philistine champion, stepped forth in battle armor. He towered three or four feet taller than everybody else. David heard him shout his challenge to the army of Israel.

Pandemonium broke out. "When all the men of Israel saw the man, they fled from him and were greatly afraid" (1 Sam. 17:23–24). Rather than fight, they scrambled to find hiding places.

In the midst of the commotion, men of Israel told David, "Have you seen this man who is coming up? Surely he is coming up *to defy Israel.* And it will be that the king will enrich the man who kills him with great riches and will give him his daughter and make his father's house free in Israel" (1 Sam. 17:25, emphasis added).

That's strange. In the midst of all the chaos, why did soldiers tell David about the reward offered? A young lad wouldn't look like he could kill a nine-foot giant. Why would they say such to a shepherd boy?

Perhaps they noticed something different about the lad. David was not dressed like a warrior—but he acted like one. He didn't bolt in fear like all those who had been in the camp for forty days.

> Then David spoke to the men who were standing by him, saying, "What will be done for the man who kills this Philistine, and takes *away the reproach from Israel*? For who is this *uncircumcised Philistine*, that he should defy the armies of the living God?" (1 Sam. 17:26, emphasis added)

The men told David, "surely he is coming *to defy Israel*." David asked in return, "What shall be done to the man that …takes away the reproach *from Israel*?" But notice David's words as he continues, "For who is this *uncircumcised Philistine*, that he should defy the *armies of the living God*?" (1 Sam. 17:25–26).

Two things in these short lines show us the source of David's courage. First, Goliath had challenged the *armies of Israel*. The men spoke of Goliath's defiance *of Israel*. However, David showed a different perspective when he asked, "Who is he to 'defy the armies *of the living God*?'" The Israelites were the people of God. Thus, the armies of Israel were representatives of God. David was the only one who realized that when Goliath challenged Israel, he was also challenging *God*. The two were one.

Secondly, when David asked, "Who is this uncircumcised Philistine?" he pointed out the Truth, "If he's not circumcised, he is not in covenant with the living God. Goliath isn't one of us. Therefore, God will fight against him for us." With one phrase, *uncircumcised Philistine*, David changed the perspective of Goliath's challenge to one of Israel's covenant with God.

God was faithful to protect David when he fought the lion and the bear. This was just another opportunity to depend on the God who was Israel's shield. When confronted by a giant, David's faith was not based on what man can do, but on what God can do.

In response to the question of what would happen to the man that killed Goliath, the men told David, "'Thus it will be done for the man who kills him.'"

Eliab, David's eldest brother became furious when he heard David's question. He turned on David and said, "Why have you come down? And with whom have you left those few sheep in the wilderness? I know your insolence and the wickedness of your heart; for you have come down in order to see the battle" (1 Sam. 17:27–28). Why would Eliab become angry because of David's question?

As the eldest son, Eliab may have expected David to look up to him like little brother's do. However, he had run and hidden while David showed courage and confidence. Eliab's cowardice looked bad compared to David's demonstration of faith. He may have been ashamed that his little brother was more courageous than he. Furthermore, Samuel had passed him over to anoint David to be the next king. Consequently, David was a natural target for Eliab's anger.

A normal reaction on David's part would be to defend himself against unjust anger. He could have explained to Eliab how his father had sent him, or that he had left the sheep in someone's care. But David didn't let Eliab's angry accusations distract him from the need of the moment. Neither was he swayed from his position of faith.

The Foundation of David's Faith

In response to Eliab's accusations, David said, "What have I now done? Is there not a cause?" (1 Sam. 17:29 KJV).

David's response carries more significance than is obvious in English. The word *cause* is *dabar* in Hebrew. It means a word, a matter, cause, or thing.[7] David used the same word we find in Genesis 15:1 when God appeared to Abram, "the word (*dabar*) of the Lord came to Abram in a vision." As we mentioned earlier, in Hebrew *dabar* includes a sense of something substantive or solid. David is referring to something substantive when he says, "is there not a thing, a *dabar*, a word?"

Look back at Genesis 15:1 briefly, "After these things the word (dabar) of the Lord came to Abram in a vision saying . . ." The *dabar* gave Abram a mental picture of something solid to cling to. David held the same vision of God as his provision and protection—his covenant God.

David is thinking beyond the defiance of the Philistine. He is asking, "Is there not a *word?* Is there not something solid we can cling to?"

In response to Eliab's accusations, rather than take time to defend himself, David implied, "This isn't about me. God has given us something substantive. God came down to Abraham and walked among the pieces. He was with Moses in the crossing of the Red Sea and with the Israelites as they wandered in the wilderness. God's covenant with Abraham is everlasting. Doesn't it mean anything to us who are the generations to come? Do we not have a *word* from God that He is our shield? That He is our protector? Has he not *always* gone before us, prepared the way, and fought on our behalf?"

In other words, "Are we not a people who have a word?"

Indeed, were they not a people who had a word? From all people on the face of the earth, Israel was chosen. They had a word, Jahweh, "I AM with you." For David, the word was alive because he had experienced it. He had a cause. It had substance and produced faith in him.

All David did was recognize that Goliath was not circumcised, refer to "the armies of the living God," and ask, "Is there not a word?" He was younger and smaller than the warriors around him, but instead of quaking in fear because of his inadequacies, he was confident in God. His words of faith were in stark contrast to those around him. No other man in Israel had spoken words of faith.

It didn't take long for news of David to reach the king. King Saul immediately said, "Get that man and bring him to me."

Goliath had asked, "Is there not a man in Israel?" Finally they found a man—but we would consider him a boy.* He was welcomed as a man because he spoke words of faith.

**Strong's*, H5288, na'ar, nah'-ar. *Na'ar* is the Hebrew word used to describe David's age. It is the word used for infancy to adolescence. Therefore, we can assume that David was probably about thirteen or fourteen years old.

David Meets with Saul

Saul sent for David to come to him. David told Saul, "Let no man's heart fail on account of him; your servant will go and fight with this Philistine" (1 Sam. 17:31–32).

> Then Saul said to David, "You are not able to go against this Philistine to fight with him; for you are but a youth while he has been a warrior from his youth."
>
> But David said to Saul, "Your servant was tending his father's sheep. When a lion or a bear came and took a lamb from the flock, I went out after him and attacked him, and rescued it from his mouth; and when he rose up against me, I seized him by his beard and struck him and killed him. Your servant has killed both the lion and the bear; and *this uncircumcised Philistine* will be like one of them, since he has taunted the *armies of the living God*." (1 Sam. 17:33–36, emphasis added)

In his repeated referral to Goliath as "this uncircumcised Philistine," David further demonstrated understanding that anyone who is not circumcised challenges God when he defies one of God's covenant partners. The one and only living God had committed to be Israel's shield and protection. What could a measly giant do to them?

David said moreover, "The Lord that delivered me out of the paw of the lion, and out of the paw of the bear, he will deliver me out of the hand of this Philistine" (1 Sam. 17:37).

Saul said to David, "Go, and the LORD be with thee" (1 Sam. 17:37).

David had a covenant mark in his flesh. He had nothing to fear. He was only a boy, but his confidence in his covenant God was so strong that King Saul released him to single-handedly fight a giant that had terrorized the army of Israel for forty days.

Preparation for Battle

Saul prepared David for battle by clothing him with his armor. He then gave David a bronze helmet to protect his head and a sword at his side. Saul was a full-grown man, head and shoulders taller than other men. David was young and still not fully developed. Saul's breastplate, coat of mail, and greaves (shin guards) swamped David. There was no way he could fight effectively in them, even if he had been trained in their use.

"So David said to Saul, 'I cannot go with these, for I have not tested them.' And David took them off" (1 Sam. 17:38–39).

Kay: Imagining David in Saul's armor reminds me of dressing up in my mother's clothes as a child. With a purse draped over one elbow, both hands were needed to hold the dress up so I wouldn't trip. The addition of high heels finished the picture, but it greatly complicated movement. I spent more time dressing up than I spent playing. The idea of playing dress-up was more appealing than wearing grown-up clothes was practical. David evidently found Saul's armor impractical as well..

However, the contrast between Saul and David is much greater than the physical. Saul's armor was just as much a misfit in the spiritual realm. Before the confrontation with Goliath, Saul had disobeyed the Lord, and the Spirit of God no longer resided in him. He measured his power by his own strength. He made decisions from reason rather than from God's guidance, and his rebellion was as the sin of witchcraft.[8] Saul spoke from a position of the flesh.

In contrast, David spoke the position of covenant faith. He was known for his worship and praise of God. This account demonstrates that he was also dependent on God, measured his strength by God's strength, and was confident that the Lord was with him.

To Saul, who was well trained in the ways of war, it seemed like David was going to battle unprepared and unprotected. Understandably, Saul wanted to equip him for the fight ahead. He offered David the best armor that was available. But David didn't need Saul's armor, the armor of flesh. Not only did he not need it, it would be a detriment to him. He was a servant of God, not a warrior.

David put off Saul's armor and took only his sling and staff with him. He chose the weapons he was familiar with. He went to the brook, chose five smooth stones,* and put them in his shepherd's bag.

*Why did David choose five stones if he was confident in God? 2 Samuel 21:15–22 speaks of other giants in the Philistine army. Maybe David took extra stones in case others came to Goliath's defense.

But the weapons are not the issue.

He did not have confidence in his strength or his weapons. He trusted his covenant God. However, even though David knew God would fight for him, he did not sit idly by and wait to see what God would do. With his sling in his hand, he drew near the Philistine.

The Battle

Goliath advanced with the shield-bearer in front of him. Then he saw David, a mere lad. The giant scorned David and said, "'Am I a dog, that you come to me with sticks?'" And the Philistine cursed David by his gods. The Philistine also said to David, "'Come to me, and I will give your flesh to the birds of the sky and the beasts of the field'" (1 Sam. 17:41–44).

After watching soldiers run and hide for forty days, Goliath would be full of contempt for Israel's army. Then, suddenly and with no fanfare, a young shepherd approached to fight? How could he see David except with disdain? He could not see the covenant mark (circumcision) in David's flesh. Neither was he aware that David had a partner. He had no way to know that he was facing the living God, not a young shepherd boy.

David responded to Goliath's threat by putting the confrontation into covenant perspective. He declared God as his shield. "You come to me with a sword, a spear, and a javelin, but I come to *you in the name of the LORD of hosts, the God of the armies of Israel, whom you have taunted*" (1 Sam. 17:45 emphasis added).

David's declaration that he came "in the name of the Lord of hosts, the God of the armies of Israel" should have put terror in Goliath's heart. It affirms that David was coming as a representative of his God.** No warrior wants to offend a god when going into battle, lest the god turn against him. However, Goliath's lack of response suggests that he was so sure of himself he didn't hear covenant references and did not realize that David hadn't come alone. Or maybe Goliath was so sure of himself that he thought he could defeat God.

**When we pray "in Jesus' name," we declare ourselves participants in the covenant that Jesus cut on our behalf. Because we are in covenant through Him, we can pray in His name.

What is important is that *David* was aware of the mark in his body. He took himself out of the way and put God up front. He didn't claim power, might, or glory for himself. He said nothing about his own ability. He knew the battle was not his. He trusted in God. He said,

> This day *the LORD will deliver you up* into my hands, and I will strike you down and remove your head from you. And I will give the dead bodies of the army of the Philistines this day to the birds of the sky and the wild beasts of the earth, *that all the earth may know that there is a God in Israel.* (1 Sam. 17:46, emphasis added)

Because we know how the story ended, we're not biting our fingernails, worried about the outcome. However, Israel did not know the end of the story. Imagine being in the army cowering behind rocks as David appeared. All eyes would be on him as he stepped forward to meet Goliath. With breath held, everyone would study every movement and listen intently to every word of the young lad. Eyes would open wide and eyebrows rise as David described striking the giant down and removing his head.

Every man would hope beyond hope that maybe, somehow, the young shepherd boy could carry through with his threats. Their lives—as well as the lives of their families and possibly the future of their nation—depended on the outcome.

David's final words, his reason for facing the Philistine, sounded through the valley. "That all the earth may know that there is a God in Israel, and that all this assembly may know that the LORD does not deliver by sword or by spear; for the battle is the LORD's and He will give you into our hands" (1 Sam. 17:46b–47).

David was confident. His life was not his own; it belonged to God. In covenant, he was committed to give his all. Likewise, he trusted God to be his shield and to fight for him. He gave God all the credit and all the glory for what was about to happen. David was more than confident. He was eager.

"When the Philistine rose and came and drew near to meet David, *David ran quickly toward the battle* line to meet the Philistine" (1 Sam. 17: 48, emphasis added). For forty days, Goliath had not been able to rouse anyone to fight. Now a boy *ran* to meet him on the battlefield. Goliath's mouth must have dropped open in disbelief. However, before Goliath could act, David lifted his shepherd's sling and flung a single stone toward the giant

> and struck the Philistine on his forehead. And the stone sank into his forehead, so that he fell on his face to the ground. . . . But there was no sword in David's hand. Then David ran and stood over the Philistine and took his sword and drew it out of its sheath and killed him, and cut off his head with it. When the Philistines saw that their champion was dead, they fled. (1 Sam. 17:49–51)

David was competent with the sling. However, if he lacked skill or strength to drive the stone through Goliath's thick skull, God would not have let it fall short. A little breath from God—just a little puff—would drive the stone home. It sank into Goliath's forehead and he fell on his face.

David cut off Goliath's head and took it to Saul, as if to say, "Here's what's left of the giant. Today, the Lord won the battle for Israel!" Israel's army came out of hiding, chased, and defeated the Philistines. They celebrated a great victory—all because of a boy's faith and Israel's faithful covenant God.

New Covenant Application

In like manner, God has proven that He is with us and that He is faithful. We have a Word. Like David's, our Word has substance.

"In the beginning was the Word, and the Word was with God, and the Word was God. All things were made by Him; and without Him was not anything made that was made. And the Word was made flesh, and dwelt among us" (John 1:1, 3, 14 KJV). Our Word is Jesus.

We all face battles in life, and the quickness—or degree—of victory depends on how well we remember we have a Word. "Faith comes by hearing and hearing by the word of Christ" (Rom. 10:17).

As people of God, through Christ we are in covenant with Him. He is with us in every situation. We don't have to go to battle in our own intelligence, strength, or power. It doesn't matter what the giants in our lives look like, our God will fight for us.

Like he did with the Israelite army, all the enemy has to do is distract us with facts that seem like Truth. We are inadequate if we depend on our own devises, and will find ourselves hiding and running from things that threaten our well-being.

"Faith is the substance of things hoped for, the evidence of things not seen" (Heb 11:1, KJV).

Our challenge is to remember that we have a covenant God and to trust the battle into His hands and depend on Him for protection and provision. Like David, when we move forward in faith, we will have victory.*

*We cannot choose or predict the nature of our victory. God's faithfulness does not guarantee a miracle or deliverance every time. Even Jesus, Who was sinless and had perfect faith, suffered on a cross. Through the cross, He was victorious. When we must endure hardship, the Lord will give grace and courage to suffer, and even die, victoriously.

David was ordinary. If you consider his youth and size, it could be argued that he was on the low end of ordinary. He was the youngest son of a large family, a simple shepherd, an errand boy. And yet, he stood firm and was not shaken when men around him fled in fear. Consequently, as a boy, he was an example among men of faith, wisdom, courage, and strength.

David was a hero because he had faith in an extraordinary God. However, His strength was not in himself. He knew he had a cause, a Word.

Today, the Word is alive in us through the Spirit. If we quit running from the enemy, fighting our own battles, and depending on our strength and armor . . . If we put our faith in our covenant God, He will fight for us. We can triumph over giants.

David fought Goliath before Jesus cut a better covenant. If he could trust God to fight for him, how much more do we have reason to trust?

Chapter 8 Questions for Reflection and Discussion

1. It seems David had no question or doubts about whether or not God would be victorious over Goliath. What can we learn from David about faith?

2. Read Luke 10:16-20 to learn from Jesus as He instructs new recruits as they learn to minister in His name.
   - How do you hear the covenant concept of two becoming one in Jesus' words?
   - How does David's confidence to face Goliath line up with Jesus' message "I have given you authority"?
   - Why do you think Jesus added a word about rejoicing that your names are recorded in heaven?

3. Read Hebrews 11:1-3 and Hebrews 12:1-3. Faith is believing and hoping in the Truth rather than facts which appear to be true. The only way to walk in faith is to keep our eyes on the author and perfecter of our faith, Jesus Christ.
   - What sins and encumbrances entangle you that make it difficult to keep your focus on Jesus so that you can run the race in faith and finish strong?
   - What steps can you take to encourage and strengthen your walk of faith?

4. Read Romans 8:33-39 and 2 Thessalonians 3:3.
   - Are you being taunted in some area of your life, making it difficult to keep your eyes on Jesus and trust in Him?
   - The Lord is faithful. Are you willing to rest in Him, trusting Him with the outcome?

Chapter 9

Saul and the House of Flesh

David has more to teach us about being faithful to a covenant. However, after killing Goliath, his life became intertwined with Saul's. Therefore, before looking further at David, we'll investigate the life of Saul. Through him, we can gain insight into common pitfalls that lead to rejecting God and His covenant.

Israel Calls for a King

Israel had it made. They lived in the Promised Land, a country flowing with milk and honey, a land of abundance. They also had a God who was committed to be with them and lead, provide for, and protect them. What more could they need or want?

Nothing, you would think.

However, Israel was not satisfied. Before the land was fully conquered, they rejected God's leadership. They wanted a king so they would be like the pagan nations around them.[1] The prophet Samuel didn't approve, so he sought God for guidance.

In response, the Lord said, "Listen to the voice of the people in regard to all that they say to you, for they have not rejected you, *but they have rejected Me from being king over them.*" He added, "Just like they *have forsaken Me and served other gods—so they are doing to you also. Now then, listen to their voice*" (1 Sam. 8:7–9, emphasis added).

Israel disregarded God's warning about the dangers in trusting in man as king. They chose to have an earthly leader rather than the King of kings, the supreme ruler. God heard their cry and did not block their wishes, even though it was not His desire for them.

> Now there was a man of Benjamin, . . . a mighty man of valor. And he had a son whose name was Saul, *a choice and handsome man*, and there was not a more handsome person than he among the sons of Israel; from his shoulders and up he was *taller than any of the people*. (1 Sam. 9:1–2, emphasis added)

Saul looked like the perfect man for the job. However, his description speaks only of external qualities. It tells nothing about his character or ability to lead.

Samuel had the tribes come before him so he could choose a king. Saul was picked from all the children of Israel, but he didn't exhibit qualities of a strong leader. "When they looked for him, he could not be found. Therefore they inquired further of the LORD, "Has the man come here yet?" (1 Sam. 10:21).

The Lord told them he was hiding by the baggage. We aren't told how big the baggage was, but it seems Israel's appointed king was crouching down in fear, lest he be discovered. The people ran to find him,

> and when he stood among the people, he was taller than any of the people from his shoulders upward.
>
> And Samuel said to all the people, "Do you see him whom the LORD has chosen? Surely there is no one like him among all the people." So all the people shouted and said, "Long live the king!" (1 Sam. 10:23–24)

A man hiding among the baggage does not exhibit kingly leadership or instill confidence. Nevertheless, the people cheered when Samuel introduced him. Were they not aware that he hid in the baggage? Maybe they were just grateful for a king. No matter what he was like, now they could be like other nations.

It's understandable that Saul might be insecure and reluctant to rule. He didn't have training to be king and had probably never dreamed of such position or responsibility. Nor did he have a righteous example to follow, and he was called to the difficult position of leading a rebellious people. More significantly, he was called to an impossible position. As king, he was asked to fill a role that was intended for God.* In spite of being chosen by God and anointed to lead, insecurity seemed to plague Saul the rest of his life.

Knowing His children would want a king once they settled in the Promised Land, God had given instructions for kings through Moses in Deuteronomy 17:14–20. However, their choice to have an earthly king was a rejection of God as their leader (1 Sam. 8:7).

It's not surprising that when he was put in place as king, the nation didn't fully support him. "Certain worthless men said, 'How can this one deliver us?' And they despised him and did not bring him any present. But he kept silent" (1 Sam. 10:27). Saul had a rough start, but God had a plan to give him a boost.

Battle with the Ammonites

The Lord used an attack by the Ammonites to improve Saul's reputation and bring national unity. "Now Nahash the Ammonite . . . besieged Jabesh-gilead;* and all the men of Jabesh said to Nahash, 'Make [cut] a covenant with us and we will serve you'" (1 Sam. 11:1).

*Jabesh is the son of Machir, grandson of Manassseh, and great grandson of Joseph. Gilead is the rocky region settled by Israel beyond the Jordan River.

> But Nahash the Ammonite said to them, "I will make it with you on this condition, that *I will gouge out the right eye of every one of you, thus I will make it a reproach on all Israel*." (1 Sam. 11:1 emphasis added)

Word of the Ammonite threats circulated in Israel. It seems Saul would likely run and hide from such intimidation. However, "the Spirit of God came upon Saul mightily when he heard these words, and he became very angry" (1 Sam. 11:6). The God-inspired anger gave Saul courage, empowering him to rally all the men of Israel and lead them to a great victory. He became a hero by leading Israel in the defeat of the Ammonites.

Three things are very disturbing about this picture. First, the leaders of Jabesh-Gilead looked to their own understanding for a solution rather than cry out to their God, their protector. Second, they offered to enter into blood covenant with non-believers.** Third, they didn't even look to neighboring tribes of Israel for help.

The people of Jabesh were in a sad spiritual state. Nevertheless, the Lord used this incident for Saul's good.

** If you are one with the one and only holy God, it is a travesty to that unity and to His holiness to then also become one with a people that are not one with Him.

Saul Becomes King

Saul began leading under a strong anointing of the Spirit. He was an example of righteousness as he led against the Ammonites. After the victory, they made Saul king in Gilgal. They also offered sacrifices to God. "Saul and all the men of Israel rejoiced greatly" (1 Sam. 11:5).

As Samuel once again presented Saul to Israel, he revealed the key to Saul having a successful reign.

> Now therefore, here is the king whom you have chosen . . . . *If you will* fear the LORD and serve Him, and listen to His voice and not rebel against the command of the LORD, *then* both you and also the king who reigns over you will follow the LORD your God. *And if you will not* listen to the voice of the LORD, but rebel against the command of the LORD, *then* the hand of the LORD will be against you, as it was against your fathers. (1 Sam. 12:1a, 12b–15, emphasis added)

Victory over a Philistine Garrison

As newly appointed king, Saul chose 3,000 men for his army and sent the rest home. He kept 2,000 at Michmash, and sent 1,000 to serve under Jonathan's command. Jonathan attacked and defeated a garrison of the Philistines at Geba. "Then Saul blew the trumpet throughout the land, saying, 'Let the Hebrews hear.' And all Israel heard the news that Saul had smitten the garrison of the Philistines" (1 Sam. 13:1–4). Saul sent a trumpeter to herald his—Saul's, not Jonathan's—military prowess. Jonathan won the battle, but Saul used the victory to further build his own reputation.

However, negative consequences accompanied the victory and fame that Saul gained. The enemy also heard the news. In response, the Philistines assembled 30,000 chariots and 6,000 horsemen as well as foot soldiers to fight Israel.[2] The Israelites were greatly outnumbered, and unlike the Philistines, they did not have weapons, much less horses and chariots.

Israel didn't have weapons because they had to go to the Philistines to find a blacksmith. The "Philistines said, 'Lest the Hebrews make swords or spears.' So all Israel went down to the Philistines, each to sharpen his plowshare, his mattock, his axe, and his hoe." Consequently, when the Israelites faced the Philistines, only Saul and Jonathan had sword and spear (1 Sam. 13:19–22).

Imagine 3,000 men armed with hoes and mattocks coming against a well-equipped army of 30,000 chariots, 6,000 horsemen, and foot soldiers. Saul's army didn't stand a chance. "When the men of Israel saw that they were in a strait (for the people were hard-pressed), then the people hid themselves in caves, in thickets, in cliffs, in cellars, and in pits" (1 Sam. 13:6).

They followed Saul to the scene of battle. However, at the battlefield, their king was not willing to enter such a battle without God's blessing, so the terrified army hid and waited. Since only priests were allowed to offer burnt offerings, they waited for the prophet Samuel, who had agreed to come in seven days to make an offering to God.

Day after day, they waited and trembled. Meanwhile, the troops deserted, dwindling to about six hundred men.* Saul's fears mounted as he compared the massive Philistine army to his shrinking forces. And yet, on the seventh day, Samuel still had not come to make the offerings.

*He began with 3,000 men (1 Sam. 13:2), added more at Gilgal (v. 4), and ended up with about 600 men (v. 15).

As he watched his troops desert, Saul felt he could wait no longer. He called his men to bring the offerings to him. "And he offered the burnt offering. And it came about as soon as he finished offering the burnt offering, that behold, Samuel came; and Saul went out to meet him and to greet him" (1 Sam. 13:9–10).

Saul's Failure to Accept Responsibility

Since Saul was not a priest, his sacrifice was an act of disobedience, a sin. Consequently, when Samuel arrived, he confronted Saul, but Saul made excuses and tried to justify himself.

> But Samuel said, "What have you done?" Saul said, "*Because* I saw that *the people* were scattering from me, and that *you* did not come within the appointed days, and that *the Philistines* were assembling at Michmash, *therefore* I said, 'Now the Philistines will come down against me at Gilgal, and I have not asked the favor of the LORD.' So *I forced myself* and offered the burnt offering." (1 Sam. 13:11–12, emphasis added)

Saul justified his actions. He acted as if he no other choice; he *forced* himself to offer the burnt offering so he could obtain the Lord's blessing. When God gave him opportunity to repent for his actions, Saul blamed the deserters, Samuel, and the Philistines. He spoke like a victim, full of fear and hopelessness. He refused to take personal responsibility.

The long wait for Samuel was a test—and Saul failed. He trusted in himself, not God. He then blamed others rather than accept personal accountability. His failure to accept responsibility and acknowledge God cost him the kingdom.

Samuel told him, "'You have acted foolishly; . . . now your kingdom shall not endure. The LORD has sought out for Himself a man after His own heart, and the LORD has appointed him as ruler over His people, because you have not kept what the Lord commanded you'" (1 Sam. 13:13–14).

Saul's lack of repentance led to great loss. However, in spite of the impossible odds and Saul's disobedience, Israel confronted the mighty Philistines—and won. In a later chapter, we will discuss how Jonathan led the attack to an amazing victory. However, first we will look at a consequence of another one of Saul's commands.

The Curse and the Consequences

> Now the men of Israel were hard-pressed . . . for Saul had put the people under oath, saying, "Cursed be the man who eats food before evening, and until I have avenged myself on my enemies." So none of the people tasted food. (1 Sam. 14:24)

Saul told his men not to eat needed nourishment. Furthermore, he cursed to death any who went against his orders. Jonathan didn't hear his father's directive. Therefore, when he saw honey on the floor in the forest, he ate.[3] When one of the men told Jonathan of Saul's curse, Jonathan said, "My father has troubled the land. See now, how my eyes have brightened because I tasted a little of this honey. How much more, if only the people had eaten freely today of the spoil of their enemies which they found!" (1 Sam. 14:29–30).

The army fought while faint from hunger and the slaughter was not as great as it could have been. Then, when the Philistines fled, instead of pursuing the foe, Saul's men rushed upon the spoil. They killed sheep and cattle and ate without draining the blood.

In this situation, Saul showed that he still desired to please God. He quickly ordered them to bring their ox or sheep to him, "and do not sin against the LORD by eating with the blood" (1 Sam. 14:24). Saul drained the blood before cooking the meat in order to not break God's command. He also built an altar to God—the first that he built.[4]

Saul suggested that they pursue the Philistines at night and slaughter them all, finishing off the campaign. However, the priest said, "Let us draw near to God here."[5] Saul had not thought of seeking God for direction, but he followed the priest's suggestion.

Robert and Kay: In 1974 a longing grew in our hearts to go to Brazil. It seemed impossible, so we tried—without success—to ignore it. We then heard of an opportunity to go for a year. With great anticipation, we made an appointment to check into it.

The night before the appointment, we realized we hadn't prayed about it. We were terrified of the thought of taking two children to the mission field without the Lord leading, so we immediately asked a group of friends to pray with us.

We didn't share what the request concerned, but each person in the room sensed something that pointed to Brazil. One wrote, "missionary" on a piece of paper. Robert went to the appointment knowing we were going to Brazil.

It seems that when reminded of seeking the Lord, Saul had the same kind of fear of moving forward without asking God—but he got a different response.

"And Saul inquired of God, 'Shall I go down after the Philistines? Wilt Thou give them into the hand of Israel?' But He did not answer him on that day" (1 Sam. 14:37).

Saul was not willing to proceed. When God didn't answer, he called all his chiefs together to determine what sin was blocking God's voice. He said, "For as the LORD lives, who delivers Israel, though it is in Jonathan my son, he shall surely die" (1 Sam. 14:39).

Everyone remained quiet, lest Jonathan be put to death. Saul cast lots and Jonathan was chosen as the guilty one. "Then Saul said to Jonathan, 'Tell me what you have done'" (1 Sam. 14:39–43).

"So Jonathan told him and said, 'I indeed tasted a little honey with the end of the staff that was in my hand. Here I am, I must die!'" (1 Sam. 14:43).

It didn't matter that Jonathan didn't hear the command, that he was the crown prince, or that he had just accomplished significant military victories for Israel. Saul had said that anyone who ate would die. He purposed to keep his word. Saul then cursed himself to death along with Jonathan when he said, "*May God do this to me and more also, for you shall surely die, Jonathan*" (1 Sam. 14:44).

> But the people said to Saul, "Must Jonathan die, who has brought about this great deliverance in Israel? Far from it! As the LORD lives, there shall not one hair of his head fall to the ground, for he has worked with God this day." So the people rescued Jonathan. (1 Sam. 14:45)

Because of the plea of the people, Jonathan was allowed to live.* However, he did not enjoy a full life. He was spared for a time, but later Saul and Jonathan both died in battle against the Philistines.[6]

*Saul also did not pursue the Philistines at that time (1 Sam. 14:46) and thus left their army to war against Saul all of his days (1 Sam. 14:52).

Saul's command and his pronouncement of a curse yielded dire consequences. It led to unnecessary weakness for his troops when they needed strength to fight. They killed and ate meat with blood, thus breaking a command of the Lord, and it distracted them from the battle. It also caused further strain between Saul and Jonathan. Furthermore, their untimely deaths fulfilled the curse spoken by Saul.

Battle with the Amalekites

In spite of his mistakes, Saul led Israel in fighting enemies on every side. He "acted valiantly and defeated . . . and delivered Israel from the hands of those who plundered them" (1 Sam. 14:48).

> Then Samuel said to Saul . . . "Thus says the LORD of hosts, 'I will punish Amalek** for what he did to Israel, how he set himself against him on the way while he was coming up from Egypt.' Now go and strike Amalek *and utterly destroy all that he has, and do not spare him; but put to death both man and woman, child and infant, ox and sheep, camel and donkey*.'" (1 Sam. 15:1–3)

Shortly after the children of Israel left Egypt, Amalek waged an attack on Israel. Israel prevailed against Amalek because Moses, with the help of friends, kept his rod raised to the Lord. At that time, God promised through Moses, *"The LORD has sworn; the LORD will have war against Amalek from generation to generation"*** (Exod. 17:16). Saul's attack to utterly destroy the Amalekites is a fulfillment of that prophecy.

Saul summoned 210,000 men and set an ambush in the valley. He captured King Agag and soundly defeated the Amalekites. "But Saul and the people spared Agag and the best of the sheep, the oxen, the fatlings, the lambs, and all that was good, and were not willing to destroy them utterly; but everything despised and worthless, that they utterly destroyed" (1 Sam. 15:9).

Saul Disobeyed God

The Lord specifically told Saul to "utterly destroy all that [Amalek] has." However, Saul captured the king and took the best livestock. He was selective in his obedience and thus led the nation into sin.

Instead of rejoicing, the Lord and Samuel both grieved over Saul's victory. God regretted making him king, and Samuel stayed up all night crying out to the Lord in distress. In contrast, Saul went to Carmel and set up a monument to himself.[7]

Samuel then visited Saul again, and Saul greeted him as if everything were fine. When Samuel confronted him, Saul once again made excuses and justified himself.

> Saul said to [Samuel], "Blessed are you of the LORD! I have carried out the command of the LORD."
>
> But Samuel said, "What then is this bleating of the sheep in my ears, and the lowing of the oxen which I hear?"
>
> And Saul said, "They have brought them from the Amalekites, *for the people spared* the best of the sheep and oxen, to sacrifice *to the LORD your God*; but the rest we have utterly destroyed." (1 Sam. 15:13–15, emphasis added)

Saul blamed others, saying, "*the people* were disobedient." He rationalized, saying he kept sheep "*to sacrifice to the LORD your God.*" Once again, he refused to take personal responsibility. Even when confronted with direct evidence of disobedience—bleating sheep and lowing oxen—Saul feigned innocence. He twisted everything to make himself look good.

Saul Is Rejected as King

Samuel responded with a direct confrontation:

> Is it not true, though you were little in your own eyes, you were made the head of the tribes of Israel? And the LORD anointed you king over Israel, and the LORD sent you on a mission, and said, 'Go and utterly destroy the sinners, the Amalekites, and fight against them until they are exterminated.' *Why then did you not obey the voice of the LORD, but rushed upon the spoil and did what was evil in the sight of the LORD?* (1 Sam. 15:17–19, emphasis added)

Most men would crumble from such a confrontation coming from the representative of the Lord God Almighty, but not Saul.

> Then Saul said to Samuel, "*I did obey* the voice of the LORD, and went on the mission on which the LORD sent me, and have brought back Agag the king of Amalek, and have utterly destroyed the Amalekites. *But the people* took some of the spoil, sheep and oxen, the choicest of the things devoted to destruction, to sacrifice to the LORD your God at Gilgal." (1 Sam. 15:20–21, emphasis added)

Saul's heart was not open to God or to the work of the Lord. God asked, "*Why did you not obey?*" Saul replied, "*I did obey,*" and then continued to make excuses, pass the blame, and justify himself.

> And Samuel said, "Hath the Lord as great delight in burnt offerings and sacrifices, as in obeying the voice of the Lord? Behold, to obey is better than sacrifice, and to hearken than the fat of rams. For rebellion is as the sin of witchcraft, and stubbornness is as iniquity and idolatry." (1 Sam. 15:22–23a KJV)

By placing his own desires above God's, Saul made himself as god. The Lord looks at the heart. He desires a heart that's turned to Him, obedient, and quick to repent. Religious rituals from a heart set on its own way are not acceptable. Saul justified his disobedience because he partially obeyed. But God called it disobedience and rebellion. Furthermore, He said rebellion is like witchcraft and stubbornness as idolatry.

It's a common sin of proud, self-focused humans to try to please themselves rather than God. Ultimately, that was not Saul's downfall. Saul sealed his fate because he did not repent when confronted. He refused to admit his guilt. Instead, he continued to justify himself and blame others.

God is not mocked. Consequences are inevitable—especially when repentance is lacking. Because Saul rejected the word of God, he was rejected from being king.

> Then Saul said to Samuel, "I have sinned; I have indeed transgressed the command of the Lord and your words, because I feared the people and listened to their voice. Now therefore, please pardon my sin and return with me, that I may worship the Lord." (1 Sam. 15:23b–25)

Saul finally recognized his sin and confessed his guilt. Nevertheless, he continued to blame the people. It seems he was going through the motions so that he could regain the Lord's favor and avoid consequences—but it was from a heart of flesh, not faith.

God sees the heart. He will not be manipulated by false confessions and pleas. Samuel said, "'I will not return with you; for you have rejected the word of the Lord, and the Lord has rejected you from being king over Israel.' And as Samuel turned to go, Saul seized the edge of his robe, and it tore" (1 Sam. 15:26–27).

"So Samuel said to him, 'The Lord has torn the kingdom of Israel from you today, and has given it to your neighbor who is better than you.'" (1 Sam. 15:26–28).

King Saul turned his back on God so he could follow his own way. As a result, he—and thus the nation of Israel—suffered. But Saul continued to think only of himself. He said, "'I have sinned; but please honor me now before the elders of my people and before Israel, and go back with me, that I may worship the LORD your God.' So Samuel went back following Saul, and Saul worshiped the LORD" (1 Sam. 15:30–31).

True repentance involves brokenness, an awareness that because of sin, you deserve nothing but punishment. In contrast, Saul said, "I have sinned; but please honor me." How could he say both in the same breath if his desire was to honor God?

It seems Saul's conscience was seared. He didn't want to look bad before the elders. Earlier, he spoke of worshiping *the Lord.* This time he said to Samuel, "that I may worship the LORD *your* God" (emphasis added). Saul made a point to phrase his request in religious terms, but it seems he no longer recognized God as *his* God.*

*In 1 Samuel 15:21, Saul had also referred to "the Lord your God."

Samuel followed Saul back as requested and fulfilled God's directive (to Saul) to kill the Amalekite king, but it was the last time he saw Saul alive. "Samuel grieved over Saul. And the LORD regretted that He had made Saul king over Israel" (1 Sam. 15:35).

Saul's Replacement Is Found

Steps were quickly taken to replace Saul as king. Immediately, the Lord sent Samuel to the house of Jesse to anoint the next king. Samuel would have chosen Eliab, "but the LORD said to Samuel, 'Do not look at his appearance or at the height of his stature, because I have rejected him; for God sees not as man sees, for man looks at the outward appearance, *but the LORD looks at the heart*'" (1 Sam. 16:7, emphasis added).

God chose David, a man who would trust Him and obey all that he was commanded. When Samuel anointed David, the Holy Spirit "came mightily upon" him, but the Spirit departed "from Saul, and an evil spirit from the LORD terrorized him" (1 Sam. 16:13–14).

After he was anointed to be the next king, David was sent by his father to check on his brothers at the battle with the Philistines. He fought Goliath, leading to a great victory. David became famous for his courage, and "the women came out of all the cities of Israel, singing and dancing . . . And the women sang as they played, and said, 'Saul has slain his thousands, and David his ten thousands'" (1 Sam. 18:5–7).

> Then Saul became very angry, for this saying displeased him; and he said, "They have ascribed to David ten thousands, but to me they have ascribed thousands. Now what more can he have but the kingdom?" And *Saul looked at David with suspicion from that day on*. (1 Sam. 18:8–9, emphasis added)

The fearful, insecure nature of Saul returned, replacing the faith shown earlier in his life. Fear and jealousy of David dictated his actions until his death. He became obsessed with trying to kill David, chasing after him through cities, and into the hills and caves. While being hunted by the king and his army, David honored Saul by being merciful and refusing to harm him when he had the opportunity, even as he stood over the sleeping king.[8]

But the Lord protected David, and Saul's life ended first. In a battle against the Philistines, some of Saul's sons, including Jonathan, were killed in battle. Saul was also badly wounded by an archer. He told his armor bearer, "'Draw your sword and pierce me through with it, lest these uncircumcised come and pierce me through and make sport of me.'" His armor bearer was afraid and refused to follow Saul's order. "So Saul took his sword and fell on it" (1 Sam. 31:1–4).

Fear led Saul to take his own life. Rather than trusting God, he was afraid of what the Philistines would do if they found him alive. Once again, Saul took matters into his own hands.

New Covenant Application

Saul is not normally considered a rebel. In many things, he acknowledged God. Sometimes he forgot to seek the Lord, and other times, he only partially obeyed, but he didn't outwardly oppose God. In fact, the last time he saw Samuel, he asked Samuel to go with him so he could worship the Lord.

However, Saul remained prideful. He was self-centered and self-dependent, seeking what he thought was best. He became jealous of David and fearful, fighting to preserve his position as king. When confronted about his sin, rather than repent, he tried to make God see from his perspective, justified himself, and blamed others. In short, he regarded his desires and opinions more highly than he did God's. He was a rebel.

Words of the apostle Paul summarize Saul's problem:

> The mind set on the flesh is death, but the mind set on the Spirit is life and peace, because the mind set on the flesh is hostile toward God; for it does not subject itself to the law of God, for it is not even able to do so; and *those who are in the flesh cannot please God.* (Rom. 8:5–8, emphasis added)

We could describe Saul as being of the house of flesh, not of faith. He was so busy trying to please himself and pretending to serve the Lord that he didn't seem to realize he was hostile toward God. It was not enough for him to know God, to know about covenant, to acknowledge the Lord, or even to be chosen and anointed to lead God's people. None of these guaranteed the condition of Saul's heart—or God's pleasure in him. Because his heart was set on the flesh, it was impossible for him to please God.

In spite of all the positive reinforcement from the Lord, Saul never completely relied on God. Rather than obey, he did things the way he thought was best. Then, rather than take responsibility, Saul justified his actions and blamed those around him. God finally said, "I regret that I made Saul king, for he has *turned back from following Me*, and has not carried out My commands" (1 Sam. 15:11, emphasis added).

Saul didn't seem to have the trust necessary to walk in covenant. He lacked internal certainty that God is sovereign—or that He is a covenant making, covenant keeping God who is faithful to His promises. We know he knew that the Lord's ways were not his ways[9] because he tried to make God see from his perspective, but he apparently didn't recognize that God's ways are always best.

Saul's lack of trust kept him from being dependent and obedient. Without trust, he couldn't follow. The two go together. If Saul had truly trusted God, He would have obeyed and followed Him.

Sometimes trust—or faith—requires being still, waiting until the last minute, like when the army was deserting and Saul needed to wait for Samuel to make sacrifices. Trust leads to seeking God for direction and blessing—then fully obeying—even when we think total obedience is poor stewardship, like slaughtering healthy cattle. It also demands that we take personal responsibility when we fail to follow God—rather than rationalize, blame, and justify our actions. When we trust, we obey and follow.

Our relationship with God is all about Him, not about us. When we're not obedient and don't put Him first, He rejects our sacrifice as He did Saul's. Likewise, He calls our disobedience rebellion.

The Lord asks us to exchange our weakness—our flesh—for His strength. We become His, totally dependent on Him—and totally obedient. "For if you are living according to the flesh, you must die; but if by the Spirit you are putting to death the deeds of the body, you will live. For all who are being led by the Spirit of God, these are sons of God" (Rom. 8:13–14).

God is with us, His children. The all-powerful, all-knowing, all-loving, faithful, living God has pledged—sworn, sevened,* covenanted—Himself to us. All He *has* and all He *is* is available to us—if we trust Him and follow the leading of His Spirit.

*If translated literally, the Hebrew word for swear (*shaba'*, *Strong's* H7650) means "to seven." There are seven key exchanges of cutting a blood covenant. Consequently, in the ritual of cutting a blood covenant, one sevens himself as he pledges himself to another.

Chapter 9 Questions for Reflection and Discussion

1. Israel rejected God because their focus and desire was to be like the world around them.
    - How prevalent is that for God's children today?
    - What is so enticing about the world?
    - What can we (collectively) do to resist the lure of the world?
    - What can you (personally) do to resist the world's charm?

2. Saul was appointed, chosen, and anointed by God to be king.
    - What led to his downfall as leader and to God's rejection of him as king?
    - Are any of Saul's failures surprising? Why, or why not?

3. Read 1 Corinthians 10:12–14.
    - When you are tempted as Saul was, have you been able to find the way of escape?
    - What does idolatry refer to in this passage?
    - Unlike David, Saul didn't seem to have a deep understanding and awareness of covenant. How could that have made a difference in his choices when tempted?

4. What effect does blame-shifting have on a person's ability to seek repentance and forgiveness?

Chapter 10

David and Jonathan: Two Men Cut Covenant

"Now it came about when he [David] had finished speaking to Saul, that the soul of Jonathan was knit to the soul of David, and Jonathan loved him as himself" (1 Sam. 18:1).

Even though blood covenants were usually cut between equals, Jonathan, the heir apparent to the throne of Israel, cut a covenant with David, a lowly shepherd. Why would a crown prince want to become one with a shepherd boy?

Let's look at Jonathan's life to see. He is first mentioned in 1 Samuel 13:2 when he defeated a Philistine garrison at Geba while leading 1,000 of Saul's warriors. Little is said of the incident, but it didn't go unnoticed. We're told it led to further acclaim for King Saul—and further animosity from the enemy. In response, the Philistines rallied their troops to attack.

Jonathan Exhibits Faith

In the previous chapter, we discussed how Israel's army hid and scattered because of intimidation from the well-armed Philistine troops. Finally, Saul became impatient and offered a burnt offering in Samuel's place, resulting in the loss of God's anointing on his life. Saul's army shrank from 3,000 to 600. The dwindling force was indicative of the level of faith and hope in the army of Israel.[1]

Without weapons, Israel faced 30,000 chariots, 6,000 horsemen, and foot soldiers too numerous to count.[2] Only the most loyal would stay. However, while trapped in this hopeless standoff, Jonathan initiated a daring venture of faith. He "said to the young man who was carrying his armor, 'Come and let us cross over to the Philistines' garrison that is on yonder side.' But he did not tell his father" (1 Sam. 14:1).

Why did Jonathan not tell his father he was going into enemy territory? Did Jonathan know his father was a fearful man and would stop him from going? We aren't given any answers, but we are given a glimpse into Saul's activity at the time. "Saul was staying in the outskirts of Gibeah *under the pomegranate tree* which is in Migron. And the people who were with him were about six hundred men" (1 Sam. 14:2, emphasis added).

Today few trees grow in the region. "*The* pomegranate tree" implies that the only tree around was protecting Saul from the heat of the sun. As King Saul camped under the tree, we get the idea he was not moving. He was not showing initiative, faith, or courage in leading his troops.

Jonathan's movement was in stark contrast to the king. While Saul was under the pomegranate tree, Jonathan said to his armor bearer, "Come and let us cross over to the *garrison of these uncircumcised*" (1 Sam. 14:6a, emphasis added). In one statement Jonathan revealed his understanding of the covenant and demonstrated faith.* Unlike his father, he was confident the Lord would protect His chosen people from the uncircumcised.

*Saul was also a covenant man, but he didn't have the perspective of one.

He also made it clear that he understood God is greater than the overwhelming disadvantage of numbers or weapons as he continued, "perhaps the LORD will work for us, for the LORD is not restrained to save by many or by few" (1 Sam. 14:6b). Instead of looking at the physical odds against him, Jonathan looked at his covenant God.

Jonathan's faith was contagious, and his armor bearer responded in faith, saying "Do all that is in your heart; turn yourself, and here I am with you according to your desire" (1 Sam. 14:7). They were set to move forward. Rather than assuming God would protect them, before walking into danger, Jonathan sought the Lord's direction.

> Behold, we will cross over to the men and reveal ourselves to them. If they say to us, "Wait until we come to you"; then we will stand in our place and not go up to them. But if they say, "Come up to us," then we will go up, for the LORD has given them into our hands; and this shall be the sign to us. (1 Sam. 14:8–10)

The Philistine Guard

Imagine the Philistines stationed in an outpost on top of an embankment. Their position was secure because of the steep ravine between them and the Israelites. For seven days, they'd been sitting around watching the enemy hide and scatter, likely hoping for action so they could wipe out the dwindling weaklings and go home.

Suddenly, the guard on duty spied two men in the ravine below. They weren't just ordinary Israelites—they had armor. In Israel, only royalty had armor. The guards were presented with an unexpected opportunity for fame and fortune. The crown prince was before them. What a victory it would be to capture—or kill—the next king of Israel. He was walking right into their hands. When the Philistines saw Jonathan and his armor bearer, they said, "Behold, Hebrews are coming out of the holes where they have hidden themselves." So the men of the garrison hailed Jonathan and his armor bearer and said, "Come up to us and we will tell you something" (1 Sam. 14:11–12a).

Israel Triumphs over the Philistines

Jonathan was not swayed by their mockery or by their pretense of wanting to tell him something. As he pressed forward, confidence rang in his words to his armor bearer, "Come up after me, for the Lord has given them into the hands of Israel" (1 Sam. 13:12). As Jonathan faced the foe, he spoke as if it were already accomplished. He trusted the God of Israel to defeat the enemy, giving them "into the hands of Israel." He took no credit for himself. The Lord *would* prevail for His covenant people.

Jonathan is usually pictured as single-handedly dueling to the death against twenty mighty Philistines. But that was not the scene as described by God. Jonathan didn't fight. He went forth in faith, and God fought the battle for him.

The pass separating the two armies had sharp crags on each side.[3] Jonathan called to the Philistines from the valley between the armies. When the enemy bid them approach, "Jonathan climbed up on his hands and feet, with his armor bearer behind him" (1 Sam. 13:14). If they were climbing on hands and feet, it had to be a steep approach. Jonathan's sword would be in its sheath to free his hands for the climb. The two men approached the dreaded Philistine garrison with no defense.

When they got to the top, The Philistines "fell before Jonathan, and his armor bearer put some to death after him. And that first slaughter which Jonathan and his armor bearer made was about twenty men within about half a furrow in an acre of land" (1 Sam. 14:13b–14, NIV, emphasis added).

If the enemy "fell before" Jonathan "and his armor bearer put some to death after him," the armor bearer must have had Jonathan's sword. Jonathan initiated the attack against a Philistine guard, but he simply walked into their midst, and they fell before him. It appears that Jonathan did not even have a weapon. God did it all.

"There was a trembling in the camp, in the field, and among all the people. Even the garrison (outpost) and the raiders trembled, and the earth quaked so that it became a great trembling" (1 Sam. 14:15). The almighty, faithful, covenant-keeping God made His presence known in the midst of the uncircumcised who dared to challenge His people. He waited only until someone stepped out in faith.

Saul's watchmen saw the enemy army melting away and moving about in confusion. When Saul got word, he told his men, "'Number now and see who has gone from us.' And when they had numbered, behold, Jonathan and his armor bearer were not there" (1 Sam. 14:16–17).

The watchmen's report of a commotion in the enemy camp alerted Saul to the earthquake and the discovery that Jonathan was gone. As the tumult in the Philistine camp continued and increased, Saul's troops were finally awakened to action. The army of Israel came out of hiding to rout the Philistines.[4]

However, the troops were at a disadvantage because earlier in the day, Saul had cursed anyone who ate food before evening. They were weak from hunger, but they feared Saul's oath. They dared not taste the honey which they passed as they pursued the Philistines.[5]

A Taste of Honey

Jonathan did not hear Saul's command to the troops not to eat, "therefore, he put out the end of the staff that was in his hand and dipped it in the honeycomb, and put his hand to his mouth, and his eyes brightened" (1 Sam. 14:27). As we saw in the study of Saul, if the people had not interceded, Saul would have taken Jonathan's life to fulfill his oath. His life would have been cut short just as he began taking responsibilities as a man.

What is significant in this discussion is that Jonathan stepped out in faith, and his faith led to a victory—victory for an army that was out-numbered, unarmed, terrified, hiding, and dwindling. Jonathan is a hero of faith, but his father didn't recognize him for his faith or his great achievement on the battlefield. Instead, he was ready to kill him for his disobedience.

Once again, we see the difference between Saul and his son, Jonathan. Saul saw with his fleshly eyes, and made judgments and decisions based only on that. In contrast, Jonathan saw with the eyes of faith—faith in his covenant God.

Two Souls Knit Together

Jonathan's name is next mentioned in 1 Samuel 18:1 after David killed Goliath. David's stand against Goliath and his words with Saul gave clear indication to Jonathan that David was a man of faith.* Jonathan's soul was knit to that of David's because he found someone with a kindred heart. He saw a man who demonstrated what it means to *walk* in faith, one who applied confidence in a covenant God to his daily life. David stood in great contrast to those who had been running from Goliath and hiding for forty days.**

*The question could be raised as to why Jonathan did not fight Goliath, since he also had faith in a covenant God. We don't know for sure, but it could be because his father would not risk letting the crown prince go before such a formidable foe.

**In fairness to Israel we need to acknowledge that most unarmed men would hide and flee from a foe that was larger in size, greater in number, and well-armed. They didn't have a chance in their own strength.

Jonathan's heart leapt. He wanted to participate with David and be part of him. "The soul of Jonathan was knit to the soul of David, and Jonathan loved him as himself" (1 Sam. 18:1).

Jonathan and David Cut a Covenant

> And Jonathan made [karath, cut] a covenant with David because he loved him as himself. Jonathan took off the robe he was wearing and gave it to David, along with his tunic, and even his sword, his bow and his belt. (1 Sam. 18:3–4 NIV)

Jonathan confirmed his godly soul tie with David; he *karathed* a covenant. All that is recorded of the ceremony is the giving of robe and weapons, but nothing more is needed for the Israelite to know a covenant was cut. If they *karathed* a covenant and exchanged robes and weapons, it was a blood covenant.

The act of Jonathan giving his robe to David was a covenant proclamation that, "All that I am, and all that I have belongs to you. My wealth, status, and place in the house of the king, it's all yours now. Even my right to be the next king belongs to you."

Jonathan's belt held his weapons and was a sign of strength. The exchange of weapons declared, "My strength and my life I pledge for your protection." He could have given just his sword, but he gave his all, even the belt that held the weapons.

To the world looking on, they were unequally yoked, but Jonathan's heart of faith was joined to David's heart. Others around Jonathan had similar social and political standing, but Jonathan chose to be one with David when he witnessed his faith in action.

Scripture does not mention David's contributions in cutting covenant. However, it is not important, because as a lowly shepherd, David is insignificant in the exchange. If Prince Jonathan gave his cloak and his weapons, it's clear that he initiated the blood covenant and made covenant commitments. Later, we'll discuss passages that indicate that David also pledged himself to Jonathan.

Since Jonathan and David exchanged robes, it had to be obvious to Saul they had cut a covenant. At first, it wasn't a problem. Saul had already brought David into his household.* At Saul's command, David sat at the table with the king's sons and was placed in command of the army. However, it wasn't long before Saul became jealous and angry.

*David was invited into the palace to play the harp for Saul. Then, as the slayer of Goliath, he won the right to marry Saul's daughter and was thus a member of the royal family.

When David returned victorious from battle, throngs met him in the streets. "The women came out of all the cities of Israel, singing and dancing, to meet King Saul. . . . The women sang as they played, and said, 'Saul has slain his thousands, and David his ten thousands'" (1 Sam. 18:6–7).

Saul was very displeased at what he heard. He became very angry and said, "'They have ascribed to David ten thousands, but to me they have ascribed thousands. Now what more can he have but the kingdom?' And *Saul looked at David with suspicion from that day on*" (1 Sam. 18:6–9, emphasis added).

Jonathan was in a difficult situation. He was Saul's son and the crown prince. However, Saul was very angry and was trying to kill David, his blood brother. "Now Saul was afraid of David, for the LORD was with him but had departed from Saul. And David was prospering in all his ways for the LORD was with him. When Saul saw that he was prospering greatly, he dreaded him" (1 Sam. 18:12, 14–15). Saul's dislike of David became as strong as Jonathan's love for him.[6]

Because covenant bonds are stronger than family ties, Jonathan was loyal to David rather than his father. Jonathan and David both remained respectful toward Saul, but when Jonathan was forced to choose between the two, he chose to protect David from his father's wrath.

> Jonathan told David saying, "Saul my father is seeking to put you to death. Now therefore, please be on guard in the morning, and stay in a secret place and hide yourself. And I will go out and stand beside my father in the field where you are, and I will speak with my father about you; if I find out anything, then I shall tell you." (1 Sam. 19:2–3)

Even though David never did anything to threaten the king, Saul's anger and resolve to kill him increased. Because Saul knew of the covenant relationship, David feared that Saul would hide his evil intentions from Jonathan. Therefore, when Jonathan and David met, David vowed again,

> Your father knows well that I have found favor in your sight, and he has said, "Do not let Jonathan know this, lest he be grieved." But truly as the LORD lives and as your soul lives, there is hardly a step between me and death.
>
> Then Jonathan said . . . , "Whatever you say, I will do for you." (1 Sam. 20:3–4)

Jonathan proved faithful to his covenant commitment by making David's needs and desires his own. He committed to do whatever David deemed necessary for protection.

Reaffirmation of the Covenant

Knowing the king was trying to put him to death, David *again* reminded Jonathan of the covenant, stressing that it was not just an agreement, but was cut before the Lord,

> As for you, show kindness [covenant faithfulness]* to your servant, for you have brought him into a covenant with you before the LORD. If I am guilty, then kill me yourself! Why hand me over to your father?
>
> "Never!" Jonathan said. "If I had the least inkling that my father was determined to harm you, wouldn't I tell you?" (1 Sam. 20:8–9, NIV, emphasis added).

*Vine, Unger, & White, p. 142. Hesed, Chesed, H2617, "loving-kindness; steadfast love; grace; mercy; faithfulness; goodness; devotion." Mercy, strength. Hesed is a covenant word expressing faithfulness in fulfilling obligation and generosity of a reciprocal relationship. (Learn more in Appendix E.)

Jonathan agreed that David should stay hidden while he discovered the king's intentions. Before discussing plans for how to communicate his findings with David, Jonathan again brought up the covenant between them. Jonathan understood the throne would pass to David, rather than himself. Therefore, he came as one appealing to authority, not to a shepherd. New kings killed anyone who might have legal rights to the throne. Consequently, Jonathan appealed to the future king for the protection of his family.

> And if I am still alive, will you not show me the lovingkindness [covenant faithfulness] of the LORD, that I may not die? And you shall not cut off your lovingkindness from my house forever, not even when the Lord cuts off every one of the enemies of David from the face of the earth.
>
> So Jonathan made a covenant with the house of David, saying, 'May the LORD require it at the hands of David's enemies.' And Jonathan made David vow again because of his love for him, because he loved him as he loved his own life. (1 Sam. 20:14–17)

Before they parted, Jonathan agreed to communicate with David through the shooting of arrows so David would know whether or not to flee. Again Jonathan affirmed the covenant before parting, "As for the agreement of which you and I have spoken, behold, the LORD is between you and me forever" (1 Sam. 20:23).

When Jonathan reported to supper, the king was furious that David was not sitting at his assigned place at the table, thus giving Saul an opportunity to kill him. He turned his anger against Jonathan for offering protection. Saul's words reveal that he also understood that David would take the throne rather than Jonathan. "*For as long as the son of Jesse lives on the earth, neither you nor your kingdom will be established.* Therefore now, send and bring him to me, *for he must surely die*" (1 Sam. 20:31, emphasis added).

Later, Jonathan shot arrows beyond David in the field as a signal to tell David to flee for his life. Jonathan then dismissed his companion and met David face to face. In apparent gratefulness to his friend and awareness of the seriousness of his position, David fell to the ground and bowed three times to Jonathan. "*And they kissed each other and wept together, but David more*" (1 Sam. 20:41).

Jonathan told David, "Go in safety, inasmuch as we have sworn [sevened ourselves] to each other in the name of the LORD, saying, 'The LORD will be between me and you, and between my descendants and your descendants forever.'" David then left, and Jonathan returned to the city (1 Sam. 20:41–42). David became a fugitive. However, his life of running and hiding from Saul was eased by visits and encouragement from Jonathan.

It was not just a formality for Jonathan to give up his position and power. He loved David as himself and was glad to see David become the next king. Although it was not customary to go to such trouble to be sure a covenant relationship was secure, once again they reconfirmed the covenant that joined them.

Later, Jonathan went to see David and encourage him at Horesh. He said, "'Do not be afraid, because the hand of Saul my father shall not find you, and *you will be king over Israel* and I will be next to you; and *Saul my father knows that also*.'" Once again, they confirmed their covenant before the Lord (1 Sam. 23:16–18, emphasis added).

The Nature of the Exchange

Look again at the record of cutting the covenant that led to such a fast friendship. "And Jonathan made [*karath*] a covenant with David because he loved him as himself. Jonathan took off the robe he was wearing and gave it to David, along with his tunic, and even his sword, his bow and his belt" (1 Sam. 18:3–4 NIV).

Jonathan's robe was a princely garment. It was a royal, one-of-a-kind robe, of soft, fine velvets and silks, in rich colors—the best available. He probably had sweet-smelling spices in his clothing to further distinguish him from the common person. When Jonathan gave David his fine royal robe and tunic, it symbolized giving all he had and all that he was.

David was a shepherd. All he had to give in the exchange was a shepherd's cloak. It was sturdy to withstand brambles in the field, probably crude and rough, much like sackcloth. But it was not only coarse, it stank. As David handled the sheep to check for sores and parasites every day, the lanolin from the wool rubbed off on his cloak. The stench of lanolin doesn't easily wash off. It permeated David's clothing. In exchange for fine royal robes, David would have given Jonathan a rough foul-smelling shepherd's cloak. What a miss-match!

For the weapon exchange, Jonathan gave David a shield, his sword, his dagger, his bow, and his belt. He was Saul's son, so the weapons were the best, and were probably richly decorated. He gave it all to David. In contrast, all David had to give Jonathan was a sling, pouch, and a shepherd's staff.

To on-lookers, the shepherd boy looked like a king. The prince appeared to be a shepherd. David and Jonathan had new identities.

New Covenant Application

This is what Jesus Christ did for us. He's the Prince of Peace. His robe is a royal robe, a robe of righteousness, pure and spotless, filled with the fragrance of heaven—the best. When He left His place in glory to take on the form of man, He gave up His royal robe to walk among sinners. He clothed Himself in flesh. "The Word became flesh and dwelt among us" (John 1:14).

> Who, although He existed in the form of God, did not regard equality with God a thing to be grasped, but emptied Himself, taking the form of a bond-servant, and being made in the likeness of men. And being found in appearance as a man, He humbled Himself by becoming obedient to the point of death, even death on a cross. (Phil. 2:6–8)

Our cloak, like David's, is filled with the things of the earth, the stench of sin—of selfishness, bitterness, enmity, and pride. It's rough, containing all things that make up the fallen nature of man. As Jesus walked on the earth, even His disciples were slow to realize that He was the Son of God. They knew him by His robe, that of man.

As we put on Jesus' robe, we put on Jesus Christ Himself. We become one with Him. We join Jesus in His life, death, and resurrection.* Like David, we also take on a new identity—Jesus Himself. We are wearing Jesus' royal robe. When the Father looks at us, He doesn't see our filth and grime. He sees Jesus, because we're in Him. He doesn't smell the stench of the world. He smells the sweet aroma of the sacrifice of Christ.[7]

*As discussed later, this is completed in baptism. Baptism (like circumcision in the Old Covenant) is the mark in the flesh that seals the new identity in Christ Jesus.

Because we are in Jesus, we can move forward against impossible odds. Like Jonathan, we can walk among the enemy and watch them fall around us. We too can know that the Lord is not restrained to save by many or by few. If we stay hidden in Him, faithful to the covenant, we can trust Him to be our protection and provision in any situation. "For whatever is born of God overcomes the world; and this is the victory that has overcome the world—our faith" (1 John 5:4).

Chapter 10 Questions for Reflection and Discussion

1. What have we learned in this chapter that is important for making a strong covenant?

2. Jonathan climbed the cliff to face the Philistines because he trusted God to fight for him, but he participated too.
   - What was Jonathan's part/responsibility? What was God's?
   - How does that apply to your life?

3. Jonathan and David reaffirmed their covenant commitment many times.
   - Why do you think they needed to do that?
   - If we are not confident of our covenant relationship with the living God . . .
     i. How does it affect our trust level?
     ii. How does it affect our commitment to the Lord?

4. Because covenant bonds are tighter than blood family bonds, when torn between the two, Jonathan was loyal to David rather than his father. How does that apply today:
   - With a married couple and their parents?
   - With a Christian child who is asked by a parent to do something that God disapproves of?

5. Read 1 Corinthians 1:30. The exchange of cloaks between Jonathan and David helps us understand what it means to be in covenant with the living God.
   - What have you received from the Lord through His royal robes?
   - What does it represent for you to give Him your lowly shepherd's cloak?
   - What can you do to earn God's favor and blessings?

Chapter 11

David, a Man after God's Heart

"The Lord has sought out for Himself a man after His own heart, and the Lord has appointed him as ruler over His people" (1 Sam. 13:14).

When God designated the new king to replace Saul, He chose a man "after His own heart." But what does it mean to be *after* God's heart?

It's been established that David was a man of faith who understood covenant and trusted the Lord to be his protection and provision. David is also the only person in the Bible whom God says had a heart after His. But what more can we learn that shows his heart was like God's?

Understanding how David reflected the heart of God will help us grasp the depth of God's love for us.

Perhaps David's heart can best be seen in Psalms where he poured out his heart. In his songs, he proclaimed praise for what the Lord had done, but he was also honest about his fears, impatience, and depression. In difficult circumstances, he unburdened his heart, beseeching God for help and strength. Sometimes he even asked, "Why have you rejected me?" Whatever the situation, he was honest about his own state, and acknowledged God as Lord of his life. However, when he was discouraged or afraid, the Psalms usually ended in a statement of trust in the Lord, such as "still I will praise you" or "I will give thanks to you."[1]

David Sought God

We can also learn of the nature of David's heart by looking at the choices he made in life. He acknowledged God as his Lord and submitted to Him. Rather than trying to maintain control himself, he consistently sought the Lord. David looked to God when he was fleeing for his life,[2] when he needed direction,[3] and when his men needed reassurance.[4] He was a strong and successful warrior and king. He "became greater and greater, for the LORD God of hosts was with him" (2 Sam. 5:10).

It seems David's life was enchanted, that he couldn't help but succeed, but, in truth, it was no more enchanted than Saul's. His advantage was that he trusted his covenant partner. He chose to depend on God, rather than himself. David's life was not blessed because of some sort of magic, it was blessed because he consistently sought the Lord and followed His commands.*

*Space does not permit discussion of times he failed to submit. Dire consequence followed David after he took Bathsheba. He no longer led a life where the blessing of God was so evident (2 Sam. 11 and following).

When David was anointed by Samuel to be king, the Holy Spirit came upon him, which did set him apart from his peers. However, Saul was anointed by the Spirit too—as are believers today.

David Honored Authority

David not only honored his heavenly authority, he also consistently showed honor and respect to those in authority on earth. When Saul commanded that David be killed and led his army in search of him, David had every reason to justify killing Saul in self-defense. However, David didn't view Saul as an enemy. Because he was aware that the Lord had placed Saul in power, he acted toward him with the honor and respect due a king.

Twice, while fleeing for his life, David had perfect opportunities to kill Saul, but he spared him rather than harmed him.[5] He told his men, "Far be it from me *because of the LORD* that I should do this thing to my lord, *the LORD's anointed*, to stretch out my hand against him, *since he is the LORD's anointed*" (1 Sam. 24:5–6, emphasis added).

When Saul, who had been trying to kill David, died in a battle against the Philistines, rather than rejoice, David wept and fasted. He asked the Amalekite who ended Saul's life, "How is it you were not afraid to stretch out your hand to destroy the LORD's anointed?" (2 Sam. 1:14). David then executed the Amalekite for killing the king, and called the nation of Judah to mourn.

David Gave God the Glory

David did not seek position or honor. From the time he was anointed, he knew he would *some day* be king, but he did nothing to rush it. Even when he was seated on the throne of a united Israel, he didn't take any glory for himself. He realized that it was the work of God, for the name of God, and for the people of God.[6]

As mentioned, praise and transparency in worship, as well as seeking, honoring, and giving God glory all flow from a heart after God's heart. However, David offers further evidence that he had a heart like God's. His actions toward Jonathan's offspring show covenant faithfulness that is like God's. They also help us understand God's love toward us. We can gain better understanding of what it means to have a heart after God's by looking more closely at this time in David's life.

David Remembered His Covenant Commitment

After coming to the throne, David spent years unifying the tribes of Israel and fighting adjacent nations that were warring against them. "And the Lord helped David wherever he went" (2 Sam. 8:6b). He defeated the Jebusites, Moabites, Edomites, the Philistines, the Ammonites, the Arameans, the Amalekites, and more, claiming the land for Israel and for his God.

Though David spent years consolidating the kingdom, he did not forget his covenant with Jonathan and the promises he'd made to him. He had Jonathan's armor and probably a mark on his wrist as reminders of their friendship. The day came, that David made inquiry concerning that covenant.

> David said, "Is there yet anyone left of the house of Saul, that I may show him kindness for Jonathan's sake?"
>
> Now there was a servant of the house of Saul whose name was Ziba, and they called him to David; and the king said to him, "Are you Ziba?"
>
> And he said, "I am your servant."
>
> And the king said, "Is there not yet anyone of the house of Saul to whom I may show the kindness of God?"
>
> And Ziba said to the king, "There is still a son of Jonathan who is crippled in both feet." (2 Sam. 9:1–3)

What does Scripture tell us about this son who was crippled in both feet? We find the account in 2 Samuel 4:4, "Now Jonathan, Saul's son, had a son crippled in his feet. He was five years old when the report of Saul and Jonathan came from Jezreel, and his nurse took him up and fled. It happened that in her hurry to flee, he fell and became lame."

We can imagine the scene. The nurse heard that Saul and Jonathan were both killed in battle. With the king and crown prince dead, the next in line, Jonathan's son, Mephibosheth, would be the subsequent target of anyone who hoped to take the throne in Saul's place.

Even if Israel's army kept the Philistines at bay, Mephibosheth was still not safe because it was expected that David would become king. Traditionally, anyone who became king would slay all those who might have some claim to the throne. David would surely kill the crown prince in order to have full title as king. Since it was the nurse's duty to care for the next in line, her only thought would be to get him to safety.

The child was in jeopardy, so the nurse fled, taking the crown prince with her. While we don't have a full account of what happened, we do know there was an accident and he fell and hurt his legs.

They journeyed for several days to a place in the wilderness called Lo-debar. The trip was probably extended by the perceived need to hide as they traveled. Survival was more important than straight legs. Consequently, Mephibosheth's legs were never properly set and he became crippled.

Instead of growing up as a prince in the house of the king, Mephibosheth lived the life of a fugitive, hiding out in the wilderness, away from his inheritance and what seemed to be his rightful position as king. Life was hard. Unable to get around on his own, he couldn't run and play games with other boys. He may have even been dependent on others to help with much of his basic care.

What reason would be given to Mephibosheth to explain why he was lame and living as a fugitive? As a descendent of King Saul, he should be king, not David. David would be the natural one to blame. Surely it was David's fault that Mephibosheth was crippled and living the life of a fugitive . . . because David stole the throne from him.

Later we learn that Mephibosheth was not the only one still alive. There were other members of the house of Saul, including seven of Saul's sons. Saul had broken an ungodly* covenant that Joshua had made with the Gibeonites, resulting in a curse. Later, in order to break the curse, David was forced to release seven of Saul's sons to the Gibeonites as a ransom.[7] If Saul had other heirs, why would Ziba give David just one name? Why only mention Mephibosheth?

*The covenant was ungodly because they joined themselves with non-believers, thus being disobedient to God.

Mephibosheth was Jonathan's son, the heir to the throne. But Mephibosheth was lame. If he were killed, it wouldn't be a great loss. After all, he had to be cared for all the time. He couldn't fight, work, or stand as a leader. After many years in the wilderness, Mephibosheth may have been very angry and bitter, making him a difficult and demanding young man.

We aren't told why Ziba only mentioned Mephibosheth when David inquired about heirs. However, we might surmise that Ziba didn't dare disclose the location of the able-bodied heirs to the throne until he saw how Mephibosheth was treated. He may have moved the cripple forward as a pawn, a sacrifice to test David's response, to see if he would be true to his word to treat Mephibosheth kindly.

David Acted Covenantally

Imagine with me what might have happened. When he learned of the whereabouts of Jonathan's son, David likely sent a chariot to bring him to the palace. Of course, chariot or not, Mephibosheth had no way of knowing David's intentions toward him. While hiding all those years, he would naturally assume that if the king ever found out about him, he would kill him.

Then, one day he looked up and saw a chariot coming.

Only the king had chariots. Mephibosheth must have frozen. He couldn't run or fight. Rising uncertainty would likely overwhelm him. There was nothing he could do. His greatest fears were becoming reality. He had been found. His life was over.

But Mephibosheth wasn't killed. Instead, he was whisked away in the chariot, leaving his world behind. "King David . . . brought him from the house of Machir the son of Ammiel, from Lo-debar" (2 Sam. 9:5–6a).

When he was taken to the palace instead of being killed at Lodebar, Mephibosheth could only assume that he was being taken back to provide a public spectacle. In front of all of Israel, David would establish the fact that he was king, and that all pretenders to the throne would be mocked and killed.

Oh, if he had only been killed at Lo-debar! "Mephibosheth, the son of Jonathan the son of Saul, came to David and fell on his face and prostrated himself."

David said, "Mephibosheth . . ." (2 Sam. 9:6a).

The helpless cripple had been in hiding from David for years. With pounding heart, stuttering tongue, and tentative voice, he said, "Here is your servant" (2 Sam. 9:6b).

"David said to him, 'Do not fear, for I will surely show kindness to you for the sake of your father Jonathan'" (2 Sam. 9:7a).

Mephibosheth's mind must have gone wild. Perhaps his thoughts included, "What do you mean 'show me kindness for Jonathan's sake'? My father is dead. He was killed in battle years ago. Why would you do anything for his sake? You're on the throne in his place. Kindness! The kindest thing you could do now is to quit taunting me and finish the job!"

But David didn't stop there. He continued, "and will restore to you all the land of your grandfather Saul; and you shall eat at my table regularly" (2 Sam. 9:7b).

David was inviting Mephibosheth to the special table for all his sons. The king's sons were served the best food, the choice meats, the freshest vegetables, all the best—because they might one day be king. David was saying, "Mephibosheth, I want you to be as my son and to be trained in the ways of the court, because some day you could become king."

Mephibosheth's Choice

It may have been too much for Mephibosheth to comprehend. He was likely filled with bitterness, deception, and fear. Yet, David showed no hostility toward him. His gestures were open and genuine. His voice was kind, caring, and sincere. The king on the throne didn't fit the picture of David that Mephibosheth had lived with for years.

"Again he prostrated himself and said, "What is your servant, that you should regard a dead dog like me?" (2 Sam. 9:8). In Jerusalem, dead dogs were taken outside the city to a special dump, called Gehenna, a picture of hell. A fire burned day and night, consuming the trash of the city. Dead dogs were thrown into the cauldron of Gehenna.

Continue to imagine with me. Mephibosheth may have been thinking, "Don't you understand how bitter and angry my heart is toward you? All my life I've hated you because of my crippled legs and misery. David, I'm a dead dog. I'm trash. Don't you understand that I stink? Why keep a dead dog? Why should I sit at your table? I should be taken out to Gehenna, thrown on the heap, and burned."

All those years, while Mephibosheth was in exile, David was seeing the mark on his arm, remembering Jonathan, his promise, and the covenant he had cut. But Mephibosheth wasn't there when Jonathan and David cut covenant. Perhaps, seeing his confusion, David called to Mephibosheth, pointed to the scar on his wrist and asked, "What is that?"

Mephibosheth would have glanced down, "Why, it's the mark of a covenant."

"Mephibosheth, your father had a mark like this on his arm. He and I were blood brothers. It doesn't matter who you are, or what you are. I am doing this for your father's sake. God witnessed the cutting of the covenant—and is witness to how I treat you. I'm not showing you kindness for your sake—I am doing it because I loved your father. I've been longing to show you kindness. Do you understand, Mephibosheth? I love you as if you were your father, because he was my blood brother."

Can you imagine the turmoil in Mephibosheth as he tried to reconcile being lovingly embraced as part of David's family with his years in exile in the wilderness? Imagine David pointing out to him, "See that bow, and sword, and shield? Your father gave those to me. In exchange, I gave him my sling. He committed his life for me, and I've committed my life for you."

"See that robe?" David might continue. "He took my shepherd's cloak, and I took his royal robe. We joined each other, becoming one person with two expressions. You see, Mephibosheth, it has nothing to do with you. It's about a commitment I made to your father before you were born. Now, you have his privileges; *you* have *his* place."

> Then the king called Saul's servant Ziba, and said to him, "All that belonged to Saul and to all his house I have given to your master's grandson. And you and your sons and your servants shall cultivate the land for him, and you shall bring in the produce so that your master's grandson may have food; nevertheless Mephibosheth your master's grandson shall eat at my table regularly." Now Ziba had fifteen sons and twenty servants. (2 Sam. 9:10)

The king had spoken. It was settled. It didn't matter whether or not Mephibosheth understood how it could be true. David gave him a house, servants, and a place in the royal family. Technically it was all Mephibosheth's. However, the house and servants would not truly be his until he moved in.

Mephibosheth had to accept his newfound relationship with David. Enjoying his place in the royal family was dependent upon his receiving it from David. After so many years, it would take a choice on his part to say, "I'm undeserving. Thank you for your mercy."

Mephibosheth accepted David's gracious gift, but there was one thing he still had to do. He had to change his attitude and die to himself to become part of what David was offering. His heart and mind needed to be transformed before he could embrace being part of the king's household.

He could no longer think and live as a fugitive. If he had ever thought that David might kill him, he needed to change his thinking. He was now part of the royal family. He had to die to his old ways—and his old identity—in order for him to truly enjoy David's offer. Mephibosheth had to choose to be a son to David, to be one with him like his father was.

He Did It All

What if somebody from Lo-debar came to visit and saw Mephibosheth sitting at the king's table? Imagine him approaching the table, saying, "Mephibosheth, I know you. You don't deserve to be here. I can't believe you have the gall to sit here and eat at the king's table!"

Mephibosheth would have to agree. All he could say is, "You're right. I got a raw deal because I was displaced by David, and I've hated my life. I don't deserve to be here. I deserve to die. But you know what? I'm not at the king's table because of anything I've done. Look at David's wrist as he reaches for that bowl. See the mark? My dad had a mark on his wrist too. I'm sitting here because my dad cut a covenant with David. Because of him, I'm no longer a fugitive. I'm a new person. I'm a son of the king. I enjoy the life and blessings of a prince."

Mephibosheth sat at the table because of Jonathan. Nothing he could do would lessen David's love for his covenant brother, and thus for him. Mephibosheth didn't do anything—couldn't do anything—to earn a place. It was all his because his father and David had cut a covenant.

New Covenant Application

David's actions toward Mephibosheth are a picture of our Father's love to us through Jesus Christ. David demonstrated covenant faithfulness by freely welcoming Mephibosheth as his own son—by inviting him to sit at his table. He proved he was a man after God's heart by being faithful to the covenant and acting covenantally toward the undeserving.

Like Mephibosheth, we are lame, confused, and unworthy—stinking dead dogs, fit only for Gehenna. But, because of Christ Jesus, our Heavenly Father has set a place at His table for us. We don't deserve it. We can never get righteous enough or do enough good things, and never change our thinking enough, or be perfect enough to gain access to the King's presence. Never.

It's all because of Jesus. It's a gift. The Apostle Paul says, "It is not by any works of righteousness, which we have done, but according to his mercy he saved us" (Titus 3:5 KJV).

Through Jesus, God did everything we need for life and godliness. Jesus cut a covenant with His Father. If we believe and receive, we are part of that covenant. To as many as receive Him, He gave the power to become the sons of God[8] and to eat at His table forever.

Nothing you and I can do will make God love Jesus Christ less. Nothing. Jesus is sitting at the right hand of God. His place at the table is secure. Because we are one in Him, our place is secure. His shed blood reserves our place at the table.

Satan will come to you and me and say, "You! You play like you're a Christian! I know what you're thinking! I know what you've done. You're rotten! You don't deserve this."

Accusations come, and you know he's right. You don't deserve God's love. What can you say?

"You're right! I've had rotten thoughts. I was bitter. I've even done rotten things. But, look at Jesus' hands. See those marks? I'm not here at the king's table because of anything I've done, but because of Jesus. See the marks in His side and on His head? He did it all. He died for me. He shed His blood so that all who believe in Him can have everlasting life. I'm in His family. That's why I'm included in the family of God. I have a place at the King's table because of Jesus."

Because of Jesus, we can say, "I believe. I'm tired of living in my stench in the wilderness. I want to sit at the King's table and be part of His household." Jesus has done it all—because of His great love.

However, like Mephibosheth, in order to enjoy fellowship with the Lord around the table, we must die to ourselves—to our identity, our former way of living and seeing God. We no longer live as fugitives, hiding out in the wilderness. We have no reason to carry fears, bitterness, blame, and distrust. We are children of the King of all kings.

David's actions toward Mephibosheth reveal the heart of God. They tell us why David was truly a man after God's own heart and illustrate God's love for us.

Chapter 11 Questions for Reflection and Discussion

1. List the characteristics you see in David that exemplify a person that is after God's heart.

2. We are Mephibosheths. Through no fault of his own, Mephibosheth was crippled, stripped of his position of crown prince, and forced to live as an outcast.
    - In what ways can you relate to Mephibosheth?
    - Have you been able to see God's hands and/or find a place of faith?

3. Read Romans 3:9–10, Romans 10:9–11, Ephesians 2:4–9, and Titus 3:4–7.
    - According to these verses, what person, other than Jesus, is righteous enough or can do good enough to be received by God to sit at His table?
    - What qualifies us to sit at the table with a holy God?
    - What must we do to enjoy full benefits as an heir with Jesus Christ?
    - Why do we often strive to earn God's pleasure rather than simply enjoying His presence?

      (See also: Romans 3:9-10, Romans 5:8-21, Luke 7:50, Acts 15:11, Acts 16:30–31, and John 1:11–12)

4. Read Revelation 3:20–22. Are you living as a fugitive or are you enjoying fellowship at the King's table?

Chapter 12

New Covenant Exchanges

In the Old Covenant, the promises of God to Abraham and his children seemed all-inclusive. He promised to be with them and provide for all their needs. Furthermore, in His Word, He recorded—for their benefit and ours—incidences in the lives of His children that give testimony to His faithfulness to keep those promises. The more we understand what is available through covenant with God, the more we can trust Him in any situation.

However, in Jeremiah 31:31, He told us "'Behold, days are coming,' declares the LORD, 'when I will make a new covenant with the house of Israel and with the house of Judah.'" Jesus "has obtained a more excellent ministry, by as much as He is also the mediator of a better covenant, which has been enacted on better promises" (Heb. 8:6). In other words, through Jesus, we can be part of a covenant that is even better than the one cut with Abraham.

By examining the seven exchanges of the ancient covenant ritual, we will recognize the fulfillment of God's promise to cut a New Covenant and we will also discover numerous ways in which it is superior to the old.

Cloak Exchange

In Jerusalem, a throng of people gave their cloaks to Jesus when He entered Jerusalem. They spread them under His donkey as they jubilantly welcomed Him to be their king. At the time, they didn't understand the significance of their actions, but it's appropriate that the cloaks of mankind be given to honor King Jesus—and that they served as ground cover, trodden under a donkey's feet.

Our cloaks are unworthy, for "all have become like one who is unclean, and all our righteous deeds are like a filthy garment" (Isa. 64:6a). Because a holy God cannot join with sinful man, we need new robes. In His mercy, through our cloak exchange, God provided more than the symbolic covenant ritual, which states, "All I have is yours." As we give Jesus our filthy cloaks, we receive from Him robes of righteousness.

"He has clothed [us] with garments of salvation, *He has wrapped [us] with a robe of righteousness*, as a bridegroom decks himself with a garland, and as a bride adorns herself with her jewels" (Isa. 61:10, emphasis added). In this verse, the picture of God wrapping us in a righteous robe is linked with that of a bride and groom—a picture of intimacy. As we lay our filthy cloaks at His feet, we obtain the potential for close fellowship with Him.

In addition, the robes we receive from Jesus are eternal. "He who overcomes shall thus be clothed in white garments; and *I will not erase his name* from the book of life, and I will confess his name before My Father, and before His angels" (Rev. 3:5, emphasis added). Once we exchange robes, we can be confident that our names will not be erased.

In the cloak exchange, Jesus laid aside His deity and took on our flesh, our identity. He left His Father's side and came as a baby among sinful men. "He emptied Himself by becoming obedient to the point of death, even death on a cross" (Phil. 2:7–8). Not only did Jesus come in the flesh and die on our behalf, He hung naked on a cross. Just as Joseph was identified by his cloak, Jesus nakedness made it clear that He was a man.

Many questioned whether or not Jesus was God, but nobody questioned His manhood. In all ways, He took our identity—but without sin.

The New Covenant cloak exchange also includes promises of provision. God told Abram, "I am . . . your exceedingly great reward" (Gen. 15:2 NKJV). Jesus told His disciples not to worry about what they would eat or wear because their Father would care for them—even as He cares for the ravens and the lilies.[1] As we abide in Him, He will provide all our needs in "good measure, pressed down, shaken together, running over" (Luke 6:38).

As Jonathan freely gave the kingdom to David, our Father *gladly* gives us everything. Jesus went on to say, "Do not be afraid little flock, for your Father has chosen gladly to give you the kingdom" (Luke 12:32). Abraham received an exceedingly great reward. We share in the kingdom of God and are seated with Jesus at the Father's right hand.

Exchange of Weapons

The apostle Paul told the Corinthians, "For though we walk in the flesh, we do not war according to the flesh, for *the weapons of our warfare are not of the flesh, but divinely powerful for the destruction of fortresses*" (2 Cor. 10:3–4, emphasis added).

In the New Covenant, our weapons are divinely powerful and our battles are won for us through the destruction of fortresses, or strongholds. However, it's obvious that we are not divinely powerful. Our weapons are divinely powerful because they are not our weapons. The Lord fights on our behalf when we are at war. He is the destroyer of fortresses.

Paul provided more insight into our place in warfare as he continued, "We are destroying speculations and every lofty thing raised up against the knowledge of God, and we are taking every thought captive to the obedience of Christ" (2 Cor. 10:5). Destroying speculations? What about the enemy? Paul makes it clear that the enemy is not our responsibility.

Our fight is to take every thought captive—the doubts and speculations that would make us question whether or not God is big enough, or if He will act on our behalf. Our battle is to put those speculations to rest and trust the conflict into the Lord's hands.

It's often a struggle to submit the skirmish to God—our shield and protector. However, when we run into battle without Him, He doesn't interfere. If we want to be victorious, we need to remember that our strength is "in the Lord, and in the strength of *His might*" (Eph. 6:10, emphasis added). As we face the Goliaths who taunt us or the Egyptians who seek to hold us in slavery, God *will* fight for us. We can depend on Him.

That being said, we do have a part in the battle. The following verses go on to tell us to "Put on the full armor of God, that you may be able to stand firm" (Eph. 6:11). The list of armor that we are to put on is the complete armor of a soldier: loins girded with truth, breastplate covered with righteousness, feet shod with the preparation of the gospel of peace, the shield of faith, helmet of salvation, and the sword of the Spirit. We need to have the full protection of God if we expect to stand in battle.

In Genesis 15:1, God told Abram, "Do not fear, Abram, I am a shield to you." Likewise, the Lord is our shield, but He is also our helmet, sword, and loin cover. Jesus is our protection in defense and offense. We attain all these things—truth, righteousness, peace, faith, salvation, and the Spirit—in and through Jesus Christ. Therefore, as we put on the full armor of God in the New Covenant, we are putting on Jesus in every area of our lives.

However, if we expect His protection, we need to be clothed in Him. These verses are speaking of a relationship, not a ritual. We can see this in the life of David when he faced Goliath. He didn't need Saul's armor because he was in the Lord—clothed with truth, righteousness, peace, faith, and salvation that came from being one with God. In all areas of our lives we need to be *in* Jesus Christ. As we abide in Him, He will be a shield around us.

When we are facing conflict, if we are aware of our covenant relationship with God, we will naturally talk about our problems with Him. Prayer demonstrates our dependence on Him. Immediately after talking about putting on the full armor of God, the Lord told us, "With all prayer and petition pray at all times in the Spirit, and with this in view, be on the alert with all perseverance and petition for all the saints" (Eph. 6:18). Through prayer we declare our trust in God, claim the protection that He promised, and release the battle to Him.

If we are clothed in Jesus, with confidence we can "*be anxious for nothing*, but in everything by prayer and supplication *with thanksgiving* let [our] requests be made known to God" (Phil. 4:6, emphasis added). We have nothing to fear. During hardship and times of uncertainty, we can rest in the Lord. He will fight for us and we can be at peace.[2]

Name Exchange

There is also an exchange of names in the New Covenant. "The disciples were first called Christians in Antioch" (Acts 11:26). Ever since the early church, those who believe in Jesus Christ have carried the name and identity of Jesus within the label *Christ*ians. We are further identified with God because we are His children, siblings of Christ, the first born. Indeed, to all who receive Him, "*He gave the right to become children of God, even to those who believe in His name*, who were born not of blood, or of the will of the flesh, nor of the will of man, but of God" (John 1:12–13, emphasis added).

> For *all who are being led by the Spirit* of God, these *are sons of God.* For you have not received a spirit of slavery leading to fear again, but you have received a spirit of *adoption as sons* by which we cry out, "Abba! Father!" The Spirit Himself bears witness with our spirit that we are children of God, *and if children, heirs also, heirs of God and fellow heirs with Christ.* (Rom. 8:14–17, emphasis added)

As joint heirs with Jesus, we are entitled to all that is His. All our provision comes from Him and through Him. We can "write checks" on His bank account. When we have needs and pray "in Jesus' name," we are reminding our Father that through blood covenant, we are one with His Son Jesus, and are thus promised provision and protection through covenant.

Cutting in the Flesh

In the Old Covenant, circumcision was required of all males eight days old and older. Those who ate the Passover Meal before leaving Egypt and those who crossed the Jordan into the Promised Land had to first be circumcised. The mark of covenant was not optional. Because it is a blood covenant, blood has to flow for inclusion in the covenant.

In cutting the New Covenant, Jesus was our representative. His blood sealed the pact. However, He didn't make a simple cut and drip a little blood, as is common in a covenant ritual. Blood flowed from seven places on Jesus' body: the nails driven through His hands and feet (4 wounds), His back was shredded by the whip (5), His head was pierced by a thorny crown (6), and His side was pierced by a sword (7).

Jesus went beyond cutting His wrist to cut a covenant on our behalf. As He cut covenant, He sevened Himself for us. Seven is considered the perfect number. Many say seven designates the heaven (sun, moon, and stars) and the four corners of the earth—representing all of God's creation as witnesses to the covenant.[3] Seven is also the signature number of covenanting and the root of the Hebrew word "oath."* It is very significant that His blood was poured out for us through seven wounds. Jesus Christ gave His all to cut a New Covenant, one that is perfect and complete.[4] We can be part of our Heavenly Father through Jesus, who was sevened on our behalf.

**Strong's*, H7650, oath: *shaba: "to be complete, . . . to seven oneself,* i.e., *to swear* (as if repeating a declaration seven times)."

As our representative, Jesus did everything necessary in cutting the covenant. Likewise, as our representative, He will keep the covenant. It will never be broken.

If we wish to walk with God in covenant, we, too, must be cut in the flesh—but not like Abraham—or on the cross like Jesus. Our circumcision is of the heart.

"For he is not a Jew who is one outwardly; neither is circumcision that which is outward in the flesh. But *he is a Jew who is one inwardly; and circumcision is that which is of the heart*, by the Spirit, not by the letter, and His praise is not from men, but from God" (Rom. 2:28–29, emphasis added).

As with physical circumcision, when our hearts are circumcised, flesh is cut away. To enter into covenant with a holy God, our sinful lives must be put away. "You were also circumcised with a circumcision made without hands, *in the removal of the body of flesh by the circumcision of Christ*" (Col. 2:11, emphasis added).

Like circumcision of the flesh, ours is hidden. Only God can see our hearts. Those who meet us on the street cannot see our mark. We can't hold up our wrist to show that we have a covenant shield and protector. We must walk by faith, totally dependent on Jesus—but that is what a covenant with God is all about.

The mark of the covenant may be of the heart and performed by the Holy Spirit, but God also requires an external sign and commitment to Him as a public statement of covenant. Paul continued, "You were also circumcised with a circumcision made without hands, . . . *having been buried with him in baptism*, in which you were also raised up with Him through faith in the working of God" (Col. 2:11–12, emphasis added).

Through circumcision, the Israelites became the people of God. Likewise, through baptism, we move from the kingdom of darkness to the kingdom of light. We become part of God's family and part of His kingdom. Through baptism, we publically identify with Christ as we partake in the outward sign of the inward work of the Spirit. The old man is buried as we die to our sins, and are resurrected with a new identity. A new being is raised up who is joined with Christ in a life of faith and intimacy with Him.**

**The act of baptism, symbolizing death and resurrection, is similar to the ancient Norsemen practice of cutting a covenant. The two men cutting covenant were sometimes buried together under a layer of sod. Symbolically the old men died and the two were resurrected as one with two expressions. (Trumbull, p. 41)

Baptism does not in itself make us Christians. Without the internal circumcision of the heart, we cannot be in God. But there is evidence that baptism is *the outward mark* that identifies us as one with Jesus. In countries that are hostile to Christianity and kill those who become Christians, baptism is often the deciding factor for the fate of new believers. A searcher or a new believer is sometimes still received as family if he reads his Bible, meets with Christians, or even if he confesses belief in Jesus. Though his actions are opposed and he is commanded to stop, he is not always rejected. However, once he is baptized, he is likely to be shunned or killed. Baptism is the dividing line. It's the mark that indicates to the world identity with Jesus Christ to the exclusion of all other gods.

Blessings and Curses

> Christ redeemed us from the curse of the Law, having become a curse for us—for it is written, "Cursed is everyone who hangs on a tree"—in order that in Christ Jesus the blessing of Abraham might come to the Gentiles, so that we might receive the promise of the Spirit through faith. (Gal. 3:13–14)

The blessings of the New Covenant could fill a library, but they are all dependent on the fact that Jesus became a curse for us. If He had not paid our debt for breaking the covenant, we would be cursed to eternal separation from our Heavenly Father. Hence, the curse of the New Covenant is evident: if we do not accept His sacrifice on our behalf, believe in what He has done for us, and yield our lives to Him (allowing Him to circumcise our hearts), we will experience eternity in hell, separated from the One who longs for intimacy with us.* There are many additional blessings, but without first receiving salvation from eternal damnation, none of the eternal blessings are available.

*To enter into the covenant with God, we need to confess our sins and receive the cleansing available through Jesus' blood. Jesus paid the debt for sin. To receive fullness of life in Him, we must surrender to Him, giving all we have and all we are into His hands. In return, He gives Himself to us. Through covenant, the Lord promised to be with us and to be our shield and provision.

Two more blessings are mentioned in the previous verse. First, in the New Covenant, an invitation to be part of God's family was extended beyond Abraham's descendants. In Christ Jesus, "the blessing of Abraham" came "to the Gentiles," making it possible for more people to be part of God's chosen people. Whoever receives what Christ has done on our behalf is welcomed as part of God's family, and thus to the blessings of the covenant.

Second, the blessing of Abraham came "to the Gentiles, *so that we might receive the promise of the Spirit.*" Men of old—even God's children—didn't have the Spirit abiding in them except when the Spirit came to individuals to fulfill a particular calling. Unlike the Israelites, we have the Spirit of God abiding within to help us understand the depths of His love and to help us be faithful. For God reveals things prepared for those who love Him "through the Spirit; for the Spirit searches all things, even the depths of God" (1 Cor. 2:10). What more could we want?

We no longer have to go to Jerusalem to worship our God. We can commune with Him anywhere. His temple is in our hearts drawing us to Himself. Jesus became our wisdom, righteousness, and sanctification.

Furthermore, through His Spirit, He empowers us to walk in righteousness. He has given us gifts for the building up and encouragement of the body. The veil of the temple was torn apart allowing us to draw near. The Holy Spirit anoints us with authority and power to do greater things than Jesus. The blessings bestowed on us through Jesus go on and on. They are too numerous to list.

But we must remember: He gives blessings so He can bless others through us—that all the families of the earth might be blessed. "It is the Father's pleasure to give the kingdom to you" (Lk. 12:32), but the greatest in the kingdom is the servant of all (Mk. 9:35). The blessings are not for personal accumulation; they are for sharing God's life with others and for building His kingdom.

Memorials

Two major memorials were established so we would not forget our relationship with God. Unlike the memorials of old, the New Covenant is sealed with a constant, living reminder to help us walk in covenant faithfulness. "Now He who establishes us with you in Christ and anointed us is God, who also sealed us and gave us *the Spirit in our hearts as a pledge*" (2 Cor. 1:21–22, emphasis added). The Holy Spirit is a pledge, a seal, a permanent reminder of God's work in our hearts. He comforts, convicts, and guides us as well as reveals truth from the Father. We can ignore Him, but we cannot escape the abiding presence of the Spirit in our lives.

In similar fashion, His law is written in our hearts and minds, "For this is the covenant that I will make . . . I will put my laws into their mind, and write them in their hearts" (Heb. 8:10). With the Spirit and the law in our hearts and minds, we have all we need to live and walk in righteousness. We shouldn't need external memorials. Instead, we need hearts and minds that are sensitive and obedient to the voice of the Spirit.

Another memorial was established as Jesus celebrated the Last Supper—the Passover meal, a memorial of the Old Covenant—with His disciples. He reclined at the table knowing they were celebrating their final meal together before His crucifixion.[5] In the Passover ritual, the head of the house picked up the unleavened bread—the matzah, the bread of affliction—and spoke of the suffering of Israel as they were slaves in Egypt.

However, Jesus did not fully follow tradition. Rather, He "took bread, and gave thanks, and *broke it*, and gave unto them, saying, 'This is my body which is given for you: this do *in remembrance of me*'" (Lk. 22:19 KJV, emphasis added).

Instead of speaking of their suffering and deliverance, Jesus directed His disciples to take the bread and the wine in remembrance of Him. He established a new memorial by redefining the old. Let's look more closely at the tradition to better understand the significance of what Jesus did.

In the traditional Jewish Passover celebration, three matzos (unleavened bread) are used as part of the ritual. They are placed under a special white covering. During the meal, the middle matzah is removed from the stack and broken into two pieces, one bigger than the other. The larger piece is wrapped and hidden somewhere in the house to be found later. The smaller piece is eaten before the meal. At the appropriate time, a hunt is held for the larger piece, and a reward is given when it's found.[6]

Rabbis don't agree as to why there are three matzos. Many say that they represent Abraham, Isaac, and Jacob. However, if that's the case, why is the middle one broken? And why would unleavened (representing sinlessness) bread be used to represent mankind? They cannot answer these questions.

It would be impossible for those who began the tradition to fully understand the symbolism. To us as Christians, the three matzos represent the Father, Son, and Holy Spirit. It is fitting that unleavened matzah would represent a sinless Trinity, and that the middle bread, representing Jesus, be broken. Jesus, the Bread of Life, was broken for us.

Consumption of the small piece of the middle matzah symbolizes taking Jesus into ourselves, thus representing being one with Him. Wrapping the larger piece, hiding it, and searching for it is a picture of Jesus being wrapped in a burial cloth, buried, and brought forth later. The reward upon finding the hidden matzah illustrates new life and righteousness available to us because He rose from the grave.

Jesus established a new tradition—in the midst of a covenant meal, immediately before He was sevened for us—as He asked His disciples to remember Him. He took the bread and the wine and—in essence—said, "Celebrate this covenant ritual in remembrance of me." Covenant is about shared life. As we take of the bread and wine, we celebrate life together. We remember that we are in Him, and He is in us. We affirm covenant.

Covenant Meal

The Passover/memorial meal is obviously also the covenant meal, but let's back up and look at an incident in Jesus' life before the meal took place.

While in Capernaum, Jesus identified Himself to the multitude as the Bread of Life. He went on to explain to them that anyone who eats of this bread will not die.[7] His comments led to arguing among the Jews. In response, Jesus gave further explanation in the synagogue:

> Truly, truly, I say to you, unless you eat the flesh of the Son of Man and drink His blood, you have no life in yourselves. He who eats My flesh and drinks My blood has eternal life, and I will raise him up on the last day. For My flesh is true food, and My blood is true drink. *He who eats My flesh and drinks My blood abides in Me, and I in him.* (John 6:53–56, emphasis added)

Jesus' reference to eating flesh and drinking blood is covenant talk. He reinforced the covenant concept by speaking of abiding in Him and Him abiding in us. He was clearly inviting the people to a covenant celebration. Notice that there were no questions from the crowd about what He meant. They understood the implications of His words, said it was hard, and asked, "Who can listen to it?" They seemed to feel He had gone too far in what He was asking.

Afterward, when His followers were grumbling over His statements, Jesus asked, "Does this cause you to stumble?" (v. 61). We're later told, "As a result of this many of His disciples withdrew, and were not walking with Him anymore" (John 6:61, 66).

They stumbled and withdrew because they understood covenant terminology.* If they wanted to continue walking with Him, it would require them to commit everything they had and everything they were to Him. That commitment must have been too hard for them.

*Some may have fallen away because He said the Father had sent Him, and that they could have eternal life. That may have been too far beyond their comprehension.

It's easy to follow a man who is wise, compassionate, speaks words of life, and has authority. It's exciting to be identified with someone who is interesting, draws crowds, and performs miracles. Following Jesus is not difficult—to a point. However, when He asks for a commitment of "everything I have and everything I am," that's another matter. Many people draw the line before making such a commitment. Consequently, when He spoke of covenant, many of His disciples withdrew.

Later, Jesus gathered with His twelve disciples to celebrate the Passover meal.

And while they were eating, Jesus took some bread, and after a blessing, He broke it and gave it to the disciples, and said, "Take, *eat; this is my body*." And when He had taken a cup and given thanks, He gave it to them, saying, "Drink from it, all of you; for this is *My blood of the covenant*, which is poured out for many for forgiveness of sins" (Matt. 26:26–28, emphasis added).[8]

Jesus' twelve chosen disciples were familiar with the ancient covenant ritual and thus understood that He was initiating a covenant. They didn't ask questions when He told them to take His body and eat it. They were ready to take Jesus into themselves.

Once again, let's look more closely at the Passover tradition to gain a deeper understanding of Jesus' actions. One aspect of Israel's annual celebration, involving the cup, was influenced by the prophet Malachi, and his prophecy, "Behold, I am going to send you Elijah the prophet before the coming of the great and terrible day of the LORD, and he will restore the hearts of the fathers to their children, and the hearts of the children to their fathers, lest I come and smite the land with a curse" (Malachi 4:5–6).

Israel looked with longing for the return of Elijah, the prophet who would herald messianic redemption for Israel. Each year, when they set the table for the Passover feast, they would add an extra cup for Elijah in hopes of his appearance. In Jewish homes today, they still set a cup for Elijah at their annual Passover table, a symbol of hope for Elijah's return and thus for redemption.[9]

The Greek text tells us that Jesus picked up "the cup." In Greek, the article *the* is normally assumed. When used, it most often refers to a particular item. In this passage, use of the article *the* seems to indicate that Jesus picked up a specific cup.

Scripture doesn't tell us that Jesus picked up Elijah's cup—which would infer fulfillment of the hope of his return—but Elijah's cup would be the only one not assigned to a person who was present. Therefore, we might assume that *the* cup was Elijah's. Consequently, it would make sense that Jesus picked up Elijah's cup as he sealed the New Covenant with His disciples. As He held the cup of Elijah, Jesus would be making a statement that He was the awaited Messiah.

In the same sentence, He made it clear that He was cutting a New Covenant with them. He took "*the* cup after supper, saying, 'This cup is the new testament [covenant] in my blood, which is shed for you'" (Luke 22:20 KJV, emphasis added).

The disciples would soon be traumatized by Jesus' crucifixion, and their relationship with Him would be severely tested. Before they entered such confusion, Jesus initiated a blood covenant so they would understand that the relationship had substance and would endure.

Note that Jesus didn't need the blood covenant to ensure His love for His disciples, just as God didn't need the covenant with Abraham. The blood covenant is cut for our benefit so we will understand the extent of God's love and commitment.*

*The blood covenant is also a legal transaction. When man disobeyed God in the garden and submitted to Satan, sinless blood was required to buy him back. Because we are in Christ through covenant, our debt is satisfied through His blood.

As they ate the bread and drank the wine, the disciples knew they were saying, "I receive You and all that You have for me. In like manner, I am all Yours. Take and use me as you wish. Whatever You want me to do, I will do. Wherever You want me to go, I will go." They knew they were cutting a covenant, but they didn't understand what it would cost their Teacher. They didn't know that it would require the life of the One to whom they were committing.

Jesus' select disciples did not realize that He would have to seven Himself, becoming a curse for them, so they could have life in Him.

New Covenant Application

Just as the disciples didn't realize that Jesus would have to die, they didn't know the cost to those committed to Him in covenant. Then Jesus said to His disciples "If anyone wishes to come after Me, let him deny himself, and take up his cross, and follow Me. For whoever wishes to save his life shall lose it; but whoever loses his life for My sake shall find it" (Matt. 16:24–25).

We cannot *just* follow Jesus. He said that if we want to follow Him, we must deny ourselves and take up our cross.[10]

A cross is an instrument of death. If we follow Jesus, we must die. That means we will yield all our plans, rights, and desires to Him. If we are in covenant with Him, our life no longer belongs to us; it is His. Our time, possessions, checkbooks, and strength are no longer ours. We are all His.

The key to abundant, New Covenant life in Christ is death to self. Total surrender. As we yield our desires and strength to God and remain dependent on Him, His life is released in us. Indeed, it is the only way to true life.

When we look at Abraham laying his son on the altar, at Moses with arms stretched over a parting sea, or at David running toward Goliath, we see men who were mighty in God. They were powerful—and victorious—because they totally surrendered to Him. They sought the Lord's will and depended on His strength. They were victorious because God fought for them.

We follow the same living, faithful God—and are in covenant with Him. Like our heroes of faith, we are *in* Him and He is *in* us. How much more could He do if His people would take up their cross, die to self, and yield to Him under a New—and better—Covenant?

Exchanges of the New Covenant

Ritual and Symbolism/Interpretation	Scriptural Reference
Exchange of Cloak Promise of provision/possessions Exchange of identity	Phil.2:7 Jesus became a man 1 Cor. 1:30 He became our righteousness Gal. 3:27 We put on Christ Col. 3:10 We put on new man Lu. 12:31–32 Promise for provision
Exchange of Weapons Promise of protection	Eph. 6:11 Put on armor of God 2 Cor. 10:3–4 Weapons are divinely powerful 2 Th. 3:3 The Lord will protect us
Exchange of Names Identities joined Responsibilities shared	John 1:12 We become children of God Acts 11:26 Disciples called Christians Rom. 8:14–17
Exchange of Blood Cutting human flesh Joining two lives into one Mark of covenant Cutting of animals Death of self if unfaithful Importance of pact demonstrated	John 19 Crucifixion, 7 wounds Gal. 2:20 We are crucified with Christ Rom. 2:29 Circumcision of the heart Col.2:11–12 Removal of the flesh Jesus is perfect sacrifice. No animal needed.
Exchange of Blessings and Curses Speak blessings for fidelity Speak curses for infidelity	1 Cor. 6:11 Justified in Christ Col. 2:10 Complete in Christ Matt. 3:11 Anointed by Holy Spirit Matt. 28:18–19 Authority in Jesus' name Gal. 3:13 Jesus became our curse
Exchange of Memorial Gifts A permanent witness to and reminder of the covenant	2 Cor. 1:22 Seals us with Spirit as a pledge Lu. 22:15-20 The Lord's Supper
Exchange of Bread (flesh) and Wine (blood) Taking in flesh and blood of one another Two are joined as one Celebration of Covenant	John 6:53-58 Eat My flesh and drink My blood to be in Me John 17:23 Jesus in us Eph. 2:6-7 We are in Christ

Chapter 12 Questions for Reflection and Discussion

1. Since the New Covenant, cut on our behalf through Jesus Christ, is so much better than the Old, what is the value of studying the Old Covenant?

2. Read Philippians 4:6. During times of hardship or uncertainty, how will understanding the blood covenant help you rest in God and give Him thanks in the midst of your trial?

3. Read Hebrews 8:10, Romans 8:38–39, and Proverbs 3:5–6.
    - How does God guide and counsel His children?
    - Have you ever ignored God's guidance by not heeding His quiet voice?
    - What does God do if we don't seek His counsel or follow His guidance?

4. Read John 6:47–66. Some of the followers of Jesus grumbled, stumbled, and departed when Jesus used covenant talk. They were willing to follow but were reluctant to make a covenant commitment.
    - When you were saved, did you sign up to "be saved" (to be a casual follower of Jesus and go to heaven), or did you commit your life to follow wherever He leads?
    - As committed Christians, we still have times when we grumble and stumble when our cross gets heavy.
        i. Why do we do that?
        ii. How does it make our hesed (loving, kind, merciful, faithful-to-covenant) heavenly Father feel? What Scripture comes to mind?
        iii. How can you move forward in your relationship with Him when you've grumbled and stumbled?

5. Read Philipians 4:19 and Luke 6:38. All God has and all He is belongs to you. When you think about needs, what comes to mind? What does God mean when He speaks of our needs?

Chapter 13

Walking in Covenant Today

Through the prophet Jeremiah, God announced that the day would come when He would cut a new covenant with Israel and Judah, but "not like the covenant which I made with their fathers" (Jer. 31:31). Since our Bible is divided into the Old Testament (Covenant) and New Testament (Covenant), it isn't news that God has made a New Covenant.

But why? The Lord had been faithful to keep the Old Covenant, and Jesus, represented by the flaming torch, cut the covenant as Abraham's representative, so it had not been broken. Why then would a new covenant be needed?

Because the Old Covenant was imperfect. "For if that first covenant had been faultless, there would have been no occasion sought for a second" (Heb. 8:7). Even as God cut a covenant with Abraham, He knew that a new covenant would be needed. The Old Covenant could never bridge the gap between sinful man and a holy God.

Another reason a New Covenant was needed was because the nation of Israel rejected God. The relationship was broken. He "warned them again and again, saying, 'Obey me,' But they did not listen or pay attention; instead, they followed the stubbornness of their evil hearts" (Jer. 11:7–8). God could have turned His back on His children because they broke the covenant. He could have killed them.

But He didn't. Instead, He gave them a second chance. He continued to be merciful and faithful to His people and to His Word.

Centuries earlier, the Lord had promised Abraham that He would be his shield and exceeding great reward. He faithfully provided for all the needs of Abraham and his descendants as long as they called on Him. In the lives of Abraham, Moses, and David, it seems the Old Covenant was abundantly sufficient.

However, in spite of a remarkable covenant, the nation of Israel did not remain faithful to God. In the previous chapter, we discussed the superiority of the New Covenant. Rather than listing further particular improvements, we will look at basic goals, or principles, of the New Covenant that are foundational to its superiority and then we will briefly discuss our responsibility as participants in the New Covenant.

As a blood covenant, the New Covenant, like the Old, has intimate relationship with God as the basic purpose or goal. However, as previously discussed, the inherent sinful nature of man continues to be a problem in maintaining relationships. Therefore, the New Covenant is superior to the Old in two important areas: its provision of (1) redemption and (2) restoration.

Redemption

A blood covenant illustrates the kind of relationship the Lord desires with us. It joins two people in an intimate relationship, creating one person with two expressions. The Lord created man to be capable of having an intimate relationship with Him. Before the Fall, God walked in the garden with Adam and Eve, enjoying fellowship at the end of the day. He still desires the kind of closeness that comes from daily walks together in the cool of the evening.

However, since Adam and Eve ate the fruit, sin has been a problem, hindering intimacy between individuals and between mankind and God. It undermines God's design for us.

Therefore, the Lord made a provision to abolish sin.

Because the wages of sin is death,[1] the only way to atone for it is through the death of the sinner. Nevertheless, a substitute can shed blood on behalf of the guilty party—the death of the one who sins is not a requirement. In the Old Covenant, goats and bulls were the standard sacrifice for sin. However, very strict guidelines dictated how the sacrifices were to be made.

Repentant individuals brought a bull or goat to the priest for a sin offering. He sacrificed it on their behalf—but it atoned only for the particular sins that were confessed before the priest. Sin offerings were sacrificed daily—but many sins were not brought to them. Consequently, God's children always carried the burden of sin.

Therefore, God instituted the annual celebration of the Feast of Trumpets. The people of Israel spent ten days searching their hearts, repenting, and confessing their sins of the past year. Immediately afterward, they celebrated the Day of Atonement, now called Yom Kippur. It was the most holy day of the year for the nation of Israel. They fasted from food and work throughout the day.

On the Day of Atonement, they celebrated all day with strict rituals and sacrifices to make amends for their sins, so they could have a fresh start. Priests went through rites to cleanse themselves, their families, and the temple. Then sacrifices were made for both individual and corporate sin. In addition, the priest laid hands on a scapegoat, transferring the sins of the nation to the goat, and it was released to wander alone in the wilderness.[2]

While the cleansing, sin offerings, and sacrifices of the Old Covenant were much better than death for any and every one who sinned, they were imperfect. Unlike today, "the gifts and *sacrifices being offered were not able to clear the conscience of the worshiper*. They are only a matter of . . . various ceremonial washings—*external regulations applying until the time of the new order*" (Heb. 8:9b–10, NIV, emphasis added).

Indeed, not only were the ceremonial sacrifices not able to clear the conscience, they were also "a reminder of sins year after year. For it is impossible for the blood of bulls and goats to take away sins" (Heb. 10:3–4). Even with full compliance in all the ceremony of the Day of Atonement, sin remained a problem, causing a schism between God and His children.

However, "He has obtained a more excellent ministry, by as much as He is also the mediator of a better covenant, which has been enacted on better promises" (Heb. 8:6). Jesus' ministry is more excellent because He "did not enter [the presence of God] by means of the blood of goats and calves; but he entered the Most Holy Place once for all by his own blood, having obtained eternal redemption" (Heb. 9:12 NIV).

Jesus is the perfect substitute to die for our sins because He was a man—not a bull or goat. He was a satisfactory substitute for mankind. In addition, unlike those whose sin He carried, Jesus was without sin, pure and spotless. Therefore, His blood purchased eternal redemption for those who enter into the New Covenant through Christ. "For I will forgive their wickedness and will remember their sins no more." By calling this covenant "new," He has "made the first one obsolete; and what is obsolete and aging will soon disappear" (Heb. 8:12–13 NIV).

No longer do sins pile up for a year, and sacrifices no longer serve as an annual reminder of sins, because sin no longer holds us in bondage. Through His death on the cross, we are forgiven.

In Bible times, if someone owed a debt and was unable to pay, he could sell himself and become a slave to cover the amount owed. He remained in bondage until he paid his obligations in full, or until all slaves were freed in the year of Jubilee. Another possibility for freedom would be if a wealthy relative chose to ransom him by paying off his account, thereby redeeming him.

In like manner, Jesus Christ paid the debt for our sin and freed us from bondage. No longer do we have to carry the burden of sin. The curse of the law that held us is broken. We have been ransomed by the blood of the spotless Son of God. We are redeemed through His blood.*

*Jesus paid the price, but in order to partake in the ransom, one must believe and receive salvation and redemption through Jesus.

Restoration

> *Since therefore, brethren,* we have confidence to enter the holy place by the blood of Jesus, *by a new and living way which He inaugurated for us through the veil, that is, His flesh,* . . . let us draw near with a sincere heart *in full assurance of faith,* having our hearts sprinkled clean *from an evil conscience and our bodies washed with pure water.* (Heb. 10:19–22, emphasis added)

The priests feared drawing near to God. If they were not thoroughly cleansed before entering the presence of God, they would die.

Unlike the high priests, we don't have to fear entering God's presence. The living God made a way for us to draw near so we could fellowship with Him. We know that through Jesus, we are cleansed of sin. We don't need a priest to represent us as the Israelites did. We can enter God's presence ourselves.[3] Once again, we can walk with Him in intimate fellowship, just as Adam and Eve did.

The Problem

So, why are we not drawing close to our God? What keeps us from the intimacy He desires with us—and which many of us also desire? I'm sure there are many answers, such as a busy schedule and too many distractions, but there is also a fundamental problem that once again goes back to the Garden of Eden.

The Lord commanded Adam, "but from the tree of the knowledge of good and evil you shall not eat, for in the day that you eat from it, you shall surely die" (Gen. 2:17). Satan enticed Eve to disobey with the words, "God knows that in the day you eat from it your eyes will be opened, and you will be like God, knowing good and evil" (Gen. 3:5).

The enemy's enticement assumes that it's a good thing to know good and evil. However, mankind was not created to carry such knowledge or make such decisions. It seems like a good thing, but for us, it is death. The Lord forbade the eating of the tree.

With our knowledge of good and evil, we waste time every day judging ourselves and judging others, considering what we—or they—should and should not do, or what others will think or say. Rather than looking to God, we act like gods as *we* set standards. We then waste time and energy trying to maintain those standards.

God's plan and provision was that we eat from the tree of life. It represents Jesus. He is the Bread of Life. He is also the Word of Life, as well as the way, the truth, and the life,[4] "for life is more than food" (Luke 12:23). "In [Jesus] was life, and the life was the light of men" (John 1:4). "No one comes to the Father, but through" Him (John 14:6), because Jesus is "the resurrection and the life" (John 11:25).

Although the tree of life represents Jesus, it is more than just the incarnate Son of God. As we eat from the tree of life, it represents life for us in body, soul, and spirit. It encompasses fellowship, friendship, intimacy, and oneness with Jesus, and thus with the Father. It includes looking to Him for protection, provision, fellowship, comfort, wisdom, direction . . . indeed, for life. Included with this life from Jesus is love, joy, peace, acceptance, significance, purpose, and fulfillment—all the qualities our souls long for.

Adam and Eve chose the knowledge of good and evil over life. As their sons and daughters, we follow in their footsteps without even being aware of it. Consequently, it is natural for us to choose to eat of the wrong tree.

Even though Jesus' blood atoned for our sins, we must constantly choose life. As we embrace life—that is, choose to follow Jesus and enjoy abundant life in Him—we will deny our natural tendencies to act as though we are gods. We will take up our cross daily[5] and die to our fleshly inclinations.

The admonition to take up our cross every day is indicative of our inborn nature to eat of the wrong tree. It also indicates that this fulfilling life of fellowship with God is not reserved for heaven, but begins on earth. Indeed, God cut the covenant with Abraham and his children to reinforce understanding that abundant life is already available. This is confirmed in John 6:33, "For the bread of God is that which comes down out of heaven, and *gives life to the world*" (emphasis added). Through Christ, today, while on earth, if we have been redeemed, we can be restored to eternal life and daily fellowship with our Creator and Father.

Responsibility

It seems that the Lord, as sovereign God, will take care of everything if we but wait on Him. However, as those who know and love the Lord, we want to respond. We want to serve Him in return. What is our responsibility? Do we have a part?

We can learn what He asks of us by looking in the Gospel of John at Jesus' response to someone who asked a similar question. A multitude eagerly listened to Jesus' teaching and followed Him from one side of the sea to the other. When they got to Capernaum, they asked, "What shall we do, that we may work the works of God?" (John 6:28).

Jesus answered and said unto them, "*This is the work of God, that you believe* in Him whom He has sent" (John 6:29, emphasis added).

The word *believe* is not strange to us. It means to apply faith, entrust, commit, put trust in.[6] To believe is necessary for salvation. We could assume that Jesus was speaking to the unbelievers in the crowd, wanting them to trust in Him. However, such belief is not limited to salvation. It is also necessary for daily Christian living. He was speaking to believers as well as unbelievers.

John reinforced Jesus' words. He was speaking to the church, to followers of Jesus, when he wrote, "And this is His commandment, that we believe in the name of His Son Jesus Christ" (1 John 3:23). Belief in the name of Jesus is our assigned work. It is commanded for all who are part of the New Covenant.

When Abraham believed, it was counted unto him as righteousness, but that was at the very beginning of his relationship with God. Abraham's life shows us that believing (trusting) is a learning process and involves action based on belief. It was thirty-five years before God asked him to sacrifice his most precious possession.

As with Abraham, learning to fully believe will be a process, a journey, and a work for us. Belief that our God is a covenant God, Who is with us and is our provision and protection, is foundational to our trust Him. As we become confident that our covenant Mediator loves us, wants the best for us, and is powerful enough to work all things together for our good, we can surrender the things most precious to us. Like Abraham, we will be able to place our "only beloved son" on God's altar.

We won't do it in order to look holy or righteous to onlookers—or even to God. Impressing others will not be our motivation. We'll do it because God asks us to. Through Christ, He is our covenant partner. He knows best, and we trust and love Him enough to obey.

It is work to maintain such belief when we are overwhelmed with trials and doubts, *or* when we are in the midst of every-day monotony. Jesus understood that. He said, "This is *the work* of God, that you believe in Him whom He has sent" (John 6:29, emphasis added).

However, we are not without His help. Through Jesus Christ, we have been restored. Because we are one with Him, we can believe—and not just for salvation. We can trust Jesus in any and all circumstances in life.

Because we are joined with Jesus in the New Covenant, we have advantages over our Bible heroes. Unlike them, we are redeemed and therefore it is possible to no longer be separated from God by unresolved sin.* Our relationship with the Father has been restored. We also have the example and lessons of Jesus to teach us, as well as the Spirit of God dwelling in our hearts to encourage us to righteousness. We can be confident that as we fulfill the mission that God prepared for us, our belief will grow and our faith will deepen just as Abraham's did.

*Sin can still separate us from God if we choose to harbor sin rather than confess and turn from our wicked ways (2 Chron. 7:14, Ps. 66:18))

Mission: Build God's Kingdom

When the Lord cut covenant with Abraham, He promised He would make a nation of him. Indeed, Israel became a mighty nation—but rather than honor God, they turned their backs on Him. In spite of Israel's rebellion, God continues to build a nation, or kingdom, through the New Covenant.* As covenant partners with God, we share in that mission.

*Unlike the nation of Israel, membership in God's kingdom in the New Covenant does not consider physical bloodlines, but is determined solely by agreeing in the sufficiency of the blood of Christ.

Jesus demonstrated how to build the kingdom when He traveled "about in all Galilee, teaching in their synagogues, and *proclaiming the gospel of the kingdom*" (Matt. 4:23, emphasis added). All who believe in Him join with Him as co-laborers in His work. We are part of His building crew. We can follow Him, "for we are His workmanship, created in Christ Jesus for good works, which God prepared beforehand, that we should walk in them" (Eph. 2:10).

God also told Abraham that all the nations of the earth would be blessed *through* him. All nations *have* been blessed by the birth of Jesus Christ. However, He desires that all nations continue to be blessed through Him. As the kingdom of God is established on earth, the Lord blesses those who know and follow Him, thereby blessing the nations. When Jesus sent the disciples out, He reinforced the mission when He gave them authority and told them, "As you go, preach, saying, 'The kingdom of heaven is at hand'" (Matt. 10:7).

Jesus' last words to us, His followers, as recorded by Matthew, were "Go therefore and make disciples . . . teaching them to observe all that I commanded you" (Matt. 28:19–20). It is not enough to just introduce people to Jesus. Part of the mission in building the kingdom is to teach believers what it means to follow Jesus, yielding to and trusting in Him.

After Jesus ascended to His Father, the disciples waited in Jerusalem as Jesus instructed.[7] Then, in the power of the Spirit, they built the kingdom. Thousands were added to their numbers as they shared Jesus and proclaimed the kingdom of God.

Motivation: Through Love

How we do the work is also important as we fulfill our responsibility and mission. When asked which of the Old Testament commandments was most important, Jesus replied: "'Love the Lord your God with all your heart and with all your soul and with all your mind. This is the first and greatest commandment'" (Matt. 22:37–38 NIV). He continued that we are to love our neighbors as ourselves and said, "All the Law and the Prophets hang on these two commandments" (Matt. 22:39–40 NIV). Clearly, the Old and New Covenant are based on love.*

*The command to love God is repeated over ten times in the Old Testament. The command to love our neighbor is repeated from Leviticus 19:18.

Later, Jesus reclined with His disciples at the Passover table. Judas left to betray Jesus. Jesus told the remaining disciples that He would be leaving them soon.

These were precious moments, the last chance for Jesus to share His heart with His closest friends; the final minutes before He was crucified and their world was turned upside down. At such a time, He would share from the depth of His heart. He spoke of things that were dear to Him and important for them to hear.

Jesus' words centered on love, and He made it clear that the foundation of the New Covenant was the same as the Old. He said, "A *new commandment* I give to you, that you love one another, even as I have loved you, that you also love one another" (John 13:34). Covenant with the living God has a foundation of love—for the Lord, and for one another. All kingdom work flows from love.

Jesus continued to speak of love throughout the conversation, but He added a qualifier to His previous statements. He told His disciples *how* to love—"love one another, just as I have loved you" (John 15:12).

Jesus' love is sacrificial. Consequently, godly love is selfless, seeking the good of others above our own "just as the Son of Man did not come to be served, but to serve, and to give His life a ransom for many" (Matt. 20:28).

Indeed, "By this *all men* will know that you are My disciples, if you have love for one another" (John 13:35, emphasis added). The world watches Christians. They may not be familiar with the words of Jesus, but they watch to see if we love one another. When we don't show love, it ruins our testimony. Christians are held to a higher standard—by God and by the world—when it concerns expressing love.

Furthermore, those who don't experience it, hunger for true love. Too often, they seek it in all the wrong places. The most effective way for us to build the kingdom of God is for us to be so surrendered to God that He can love fellow believers and our neighbors through us.

For those who are aware of their self-centered nature, it seems impossible to carry out consistent, sacrificial, godly love. However, "God is love, and the one who abides in love abides in God, and God abides in him" (1 John 4:16). If God is love, and in covenant we abide in Him and He abides in us, it follows that His love abides in us. It's not impossible for us to love with God's love. Because He lives within us, if we yield to Him, He will love through us. We *can* love one another as He loves.

The extent to which God can love through us is in direct proportion to the extent to which we truly fellowship with Him and yield to Him. As we draw close to Him, those around us will sense a sweet glow of love in us. God's love will attract people to Him.

Mode: As a Friend

Sincere love leads to friendship. True friends delight in being together. They share hopes, hurts, dreams, disappointments, and secrets. Because they enjoy each other, they make time to be together. When together, it doesn't matter whether or not they talk or whether or not they're doing something fun or exciting. They give sacrificially to one another whenever there is a need, and they do it with joy. They love each other and want to share life. They're friends.

Scripture does not often speak of God's "friends." Friendship with God denotes a very special, intimate relationship. However, several individuals seemed to share friendship with God. As Adam and Eve walked with God in the evenings, it seems to be a picture of friendship. Also, Enoch walked with God (Gen. 5:22-23). In addition, Exodus 33:11 says, "the LORD used to speak to Moses face to face, just as a man speaks to his friend." Furthermore, while the term friend is not attributed to David, having a heart after God's heart speaks of the kind of kinship that is common with true friends. All of these relationships give indication of intimacy, of friendship.

But Abraham, the father of faith, is the only one of our Old Testament heroes called God's friend. James 2:23 tells us that Abraham, "was called the friend of God."

Although we rarely see it in the Old Testament, the almighty, living, holy God wants to be a friend with us. He desires to talk with us face-to-face and to walk with us in the cool of the evening, sharing secrets. Lest we should doubt, Jesus said, "No longer do I call you slaves, for the slave does not know what his master is doing; but I have called you friends, for all things that I have heard from My Father I have made known to you" (John 15:15).

It seems unbelievable—maybe even impossible—that God would want to have habitual, intimate fellowship with humans, and that He would want to share His heart and His secrets with us. We are not worthy. We are dead dogs. Even our righteousness is as filthy rags.

But it's true. Jesus Christ called us His friends. He died so that we can be redeemed and restored, so we can be one with Him, so our joy can be full. He paid the debt to cover the curse for our sin and cut a more excellent covenant on our behalf so we could be intimate with Him.

How do we attain that intimacy?

We give our all to Him. In Psalm 25:14, God says, "The *secret [friendship, fellowship, intimacy] of the LORD is for those who fear Him,* and He will make them know His covenant" (emphasis added). Abraham, the friend of God, surrendered his beloved son to God and was told, "now I know that you fear God, since you have not withheld your son" (Gen. 22:12). Intimacy grows out of fear (fear, reverence, awe) that is expressed through surrender. Those who fear the Lord, as Abraham did, will fellowship with Him and will enjoy the intimacy that He desires to share with us. They will then know (understand, experience) the unity of covenant with the living God.

All that I have, I give in exchange for all God has. There has never been a better deal. We can't lose.

It's the great exchange, the greatest of all time.

Chapter 13 Questions for Reflection and Discussion

1. Our work is to believe. Jesus said, "This is the work of God, that you believe in Him whom He has sent" (John 6:29).
    a. Are you doing the work?
    b. What leads you to not believe/to doubt?
    c. How can you build your faith to better trust/believe in Jesus?

2. You were redeemed, bought by the blood of Jesus. What does it mean to you that you were bought?

3. Blood covenant is a path to intimacy. Are you as intimate with God as you want to be?
    a. What prevents/blocks you from greater intimacy?
    b. What can you do to improve fellowship with God?

4. What does it mean to you that Jesus calls you to be His friend?
    a. Will you open the door for intimacy with Jesus? (Rev. 3:20–21)
    b. Will you make room in your life to dine with Him and He with you?

Appendix A

Henry M. Stanley and Mata Bwyki Cut a Covenant

Henry M. Stanley, an explorer who traveled extensively in Africa, became well known for his search for David Livingstone in 1871. In his travels, he and his companions often encountered hostile tribes or went hungry for lack of food. Consequently, he cut covenant at least fifty times with chiefs[1] in Africa in an attempt to stay alive. He needed them to be his friends rather than enemies, and he needed help with provisions for his men.

In his journals, Stanley described the ceremonies with various chiefs and told of incidents when their lives were spared because of pacts that had been made on previous visits. The ceremonies differed from tribe to tribe, but had many common threads. The natives viewed them as unbreakable contracts of two becoming one.

One account of the covenant ceremony was told in some detail. In 1877, Stanley (called Tandelay or Bula Matari) fought with a tribe that he described as a superior people who fought fiercely. In October 1883, on a return trip, he encountered the same tribe (the Bangala). The "senior chief, Mata Bwyki (lord of many guns)" was about six feet two inches in height, with broad shoulders, a large, square face and a "massive head, out of which his solitary eye seemed to glare with penetrative power."

At their meeting, Mata Bwyki was probably seventy-five to eighty years old, but he stood straight, with his white hair rising above the seven tall sons who stood at his side.[2] Henry M. Stanley's report of the cutting of a blood covenant in 1883 with Mata Bwyki follows.

> Nearly two thousand persons assembled, at Iboko, to witness the "palaver" that must precede a decision to enter into "strong friendship." At the place of meeting, "mats of split rattan were spread in a large semicircle around a row of curved and box stools, for the principal chiefs. In the centre of the line, opposite this, was left a space for myself and people," continues Stanley. "We had first to undergo the process of steady and silent examination from nearly two thousand pairs of eyes.

Then, after Yumbila, the guide, had detailed in his own manner, who we were, and what was our mission up the great river; how we had built towns at many places, and made blood-brotherhood with the chiefs of great districts, such as Irevu, Ukuti, Usindi, . . . and Kintamo, he urged upon them the pleasure it would be to me to make a like compact, sealed with blood, with the great chiefs of populous Iboko. He pictured the benefits likely to accrue to Iboko, and Mata Bwyki in particular, if a bond of brotherhood was made between two chiefs like Mata Bwyki and Tandelay, [Stanley,] or as he was known, Bula Matari."

There was no prompt response to Stanley's request for strong friendship with the Bangala. There were prejudices to be removed, and old memories to be overborne; and Yumbila's eloquence and tact were put to their severest test, in the endeavor to bring about a state of feeling that would make the covenant of blood a possibility here. But the triumph was won. "Forked palm branch was brought," says Stanley. "Kokoro, the heir [of Mata Bwyki], came forward, seized it, and kneeled before me; as, drawing out his short falchion, he cried, 'Hold the other branch, Bula Matari!' I obeyed him, and lifting his hand he cleaved the branch in two. 'Thus,' he said, 'I declare my wish to be your brother.'

Then a fetish-man came forward with his lancets, long pod, pinch of salt, and fresh green banana leaf. He held the staff of Kokoro's sword-bladed spear, while one of my rifles was brought from the steamer. The shaft of the spear and the stock of the rifle were then scraped on the leaf, a pinch of salt was dropped on the wood, and finally a little dust form the long pod was scraped on the curious mixture. Then, our arms were crossed—the white arm over the brown arm—and an incision was made in each; and over blood was dropped a few grains of the dusty compound; and the white arm was rubbed over the brown [in the intermingling of blood].

Now Mata Bwyki lifted his mighty form, and with his long giant's staff drove back the compressed crowd, clearing a wide circle, and then roaring out his most magnificent style, leonine in its lung-force, kingly in its effect: "People of Iboko! You by the river side, and you of inland. Men of the Bangala, listen to the words of Mata Bwyki. You see Tandelay before you. His other name is Bula

Matari. He is the man with the many canoes, and has brought back strange smoke-boats. He has come to see Mata Bwyki. He has asked Mata Bwyki to be his friend. Mata Bwyki has taken him by the hand, and has become his blood-brother. Tandelay belongs to Iboko now. He has become this day one of the Bangala. O, Iboko! Listen to the voice of Mata Bwyki." (I thought they must have been incurably deaf, not to have heard that voice). "Bula Matari and Mata Bwyki are one today. We have joined hands. Hurt not Bula Matari's people; steal not from them; offend them not. Bring food and sell to him at a fair price, gently, kindly, and in peace; for he is my brother. Hear you, ye people of Iboko—you by the river side, and you of the interior?"

"'We hear, Mata Bwyki!' shouted the multitude." And the ceremony was ended.[3]

Appendix B

The Charges to Israel as They Entered the Promised Land

Deuteronomy 27:9–21

Then Moses and the Levitical priests spoke to all Israel, saying, "Be silent and listen, O Israel! This day you have become a people for the LORD your God. You shall therefore obey the LORD your God, and do His commandments and His statutes which I command you today."

Moses also charged the people on that day, saying "When you cross the Jordan, these shall stand on Mount Gerizim to bless the people: Simeon, Levi, Judah, Issachar, Joseph, and Benjamin. And for the curse, these shall stand on Mount Ebal: Reuben, Gad, Asher, Zebulun, Dan, and Naphtali. The Levites shall then answer and say to all the men of Israel with a loud voice" (vv. 9–14),

- "Cursed is the man who makes an idol or a molten image, an abomination to the Lord, the work of the hands of the craftsman, and sets it up in secret."

  And all the people shall answer and say, "Amen" (v. 15).

- "Cursed is he who dishonors his father or mother."

  And all the people shall say, "Amen" (v. 16).

- "Cursed is he who moves his neighbor's boundary mark."

  And all the people shall say, "Amen" (v. 17).

- "Cursed is he who misleads a blind person on the road."

  And all the people shall say, "Amen" (v. 18).

- "Cursed is he who distorts the justice due an alien, orphan, and widow."

  And all the people shall say, "Amen" (v. 19).

- "Cursed is he who lies with his father's wife, because he has uncovered his father's skirt."

  And all the people shall say, "Amen" (v. 20).

· "Cursed is he who lies with any animal."
And all the people shall say, "Amen" (v. 21).

· "Cursed is he who lies with his sister, the daughter of his father or of his mother."
And all the people shall say, "Amen" (v. 22).

· "Cursed is he who lies with his mother-in-law."
And all the people shall say, "Amen" (v. 23).

· "Cursed is he who strikes his neighbor in secret."
And all the people shall say, "Amen" (v. 24).

· "Cursed is he who accepts a bribe to strike down an innocent person."
And all the people shall say, "Amen" (v. 25).

· "Cursed is he who does not confirm the words of this law by doing them."
And all the people shall say, "Amen" (v. 26).

Appendix C

Blessings Spoken to Israel

Deuteronomy 28:1–14

"Now it shall be, if you will diligently obey the LORD your God, being careful to do all His commandments which I command you today, the LORD your God will set you high above all the nations of the earth. And all these blessings shall come upon you and overtake you, if you will obey the LORD your God" (vv. 1–2).

· "Blessed shall you be in the city, and blessed shall you be in the country (v. 3).

· "Blessed shall be the offspring of your body and the produce of your ground and the offspring of your beasts, the increase of your herd and the young of your flock (v. 4).

· "Blessed shall be your basket and your kneading bowl (v. 5).

· "Blessed shall you be when you come in, and blessed shall you be when you go out (v. 6).

· "The Lord will cause your enemies who rise up against you to be defeated before you; they shall come out against you one way and shall flee before you seven ways (v. 7).

· "The Lord will command the blessing upon you in your barns and in all that you put your hand to, and He will bless you in the land which the Lord your God gives you (v. 8).

· "The Lord will establish you as a holy people to Himself, as He swore to you, if you will keep the commandments of the Lord your God, and walk in His ways (v. 9).

· "So all the peoples of the earth shall see that you are called by the name of the Lord; and they shall be afraid of you (v. 10).

· "And the Lord will make you abound in prosperity, in the offspring of your body and in the offspring of your beast and in the produce of your ground, in the land which the Lord swore to your fathers to give you (v. 11).

· "The Lord will open for you His good storehouse, the heavens, to give rain to your land in its season and to bless all the work of your hand; and you shall lend to many nations, but you shall not borrow (v. 12).

· "And the Lord shall make you the head and not the tail, and you only shall be above, and you shall not be underneath, if you will listen to the commandments of the Lord your God, which I charge you today, to observe them carefully, and do not turn aside from any of the words which I command you today, to the right or to the left, to go after other gods to serve them" (vv. 13–14).

Appendix D

Curses Spoken to Israel as They Entered the Promised Land

Deuteronomy 28:15–68

"But it shall come about, if you will not obey the LORD your God, to observe to do all His commandments and His statutes with which I charge you today, that all these curses shall come upon you and overtake you" (v. 15).

· "Cursed shall you be in the city, and cursed shall you be in the country" (v. 16).

· "Cursed shall be your basket and your kneading bowl" (v. 17).

· "Cursed shall be the offspring of your body and the produce of your ground, the increase of your herd and the young of your flock" (v. 18).

· "Cursed shall you be when you come in, and cursed shall you be when you go out" (v. 19).

· "The Lord will send upon you curses, confusion, and rebuke, in all you undertake to do, until you are destroyed and until you perish quickly, on account of the evil of your deeds, because you have forsaken Me" (v. 20).

· "The Lord will make the pestilence cling to you until He has consumed you from the land, where you are entering to possess it" (v. 21).

· "The Lord will smite you with consumption and with fever and with inflammation and with fiery heat and with the sword and with blight and with mildew" (v. 22),

· "and they shall pursue you until you perish" (v. 22b).

· "And the heaven which is over your head shall be bronze, and the earth which is under you, iron" (v. 23).

· "The Lord will make the rain of your land powder and dust; from heaven it shall come down on you until you are destroyed" (v. 24).

· "The Lord will cause you to be defeated before your enemies; you shall go out one way against them, but you shall flee seven ways before them, and you shall be an example of terror to all the kingdoms of the earth" (v. 25).

· "And your carcasses shall be food to all birds of the sky and to the beasts of the earth, and there shall be no one to frighten them away" (v. 26).

· "The Lord will smite you with the boils of Egypt and with tumors and with the scab and with the itch, from which you cannot be healed" (v. 27).

· "The Lord will smite you with madness and with blindness and with bewilderment of heart" (v. 28),

· "and you shall grope at noon, as the blind man gropes in darkness" (v. 29),

· "and you shall not prosper in your ways; but you shall only be oppressed and robbed continually, with none to save you" (v. 29).

· "You shall betroth a wife, but another man shall violate her" (v. 29),

· "you shall build a house, but you shall not live in it" (v. 29),

· "you shall plant a vineyard, but you shall not use its fruit" (v. 29).

· "Your ox shall be slaughtered before your eyes, but you shall not eat of it" (v. 31),

· "your donkey shall be torn away from you, and shall not be restored to you" (v. 31),

· "your sheep shall be given to your enemies" (v. 31),

· "and you shall have none to save you" (v. 31).

· "Your sons and your daughters shall be given to another people, while your eyes shall look on and yearn for them continually; but there shall be nothing you can do" (v. 32).

· "A people whom you do not know shall eat up the produce of your ground and all your labors" (v. 33),

· "and you shall never be anything but oppressed and crushed continually" (v. 33).

· "And you shall be driven mad by the sight of what you see" (v. 34).

· "The Lord will strike you on the knees and legs with sore boils, from which you cannot be healed, from the sole of your foot to the crown of your head" (v. 35).

· "The Lord will bring you and your king, whom you shall set over you, to a nation which neither you nor your fathers have known, and there you shall serve other gods, wood and stone" (v. 36).

· "And you shall become a horror, a proverb, and a taunt among all the people where the Lord will drive you" (v. 37).

· "You shall bring out much seed to the field but you shall gather in little, for the locust shall consume it" (v. 38).

· "You shall plant and cultivate vineyards, but you shall neither drink of the wine nor gather the grapes, for the worm shall devour them" (v. 39).

· "You shall have olive trees throughout your territory but you shall not anoint yourself with the oil, for your olives shall drop off" (v. 40).

· "You shall have sons and daughters but they shall not be yours, for they shall go into captivity" (v. 41).

· "The cricket shall possess all your trees and the produce of your ground" (v. 42).

· "The alien who is among you shall rise above you higher and higher, but you shall go down lower and lower" (v. 43).

· "He shall lend to you, but you shall not lend to him; he shall be the head, and you shall be the tail" (v. 44).

"So all these curses shall come on you and pursue you and overtake you until you are destroyed, because you would not obey the Lord your God by keeping His commandments and His statutes which He commanded you. And they shall become a sign and a wonder on you and your descendants forever" (v. 45).

"Because you did not serve the Lord your God with joy and a glad heart, for the abundance of all things" (v. 47),

· "therefore you shall serve your enemies whom the Lord shall send against you, in hunger, in thirst, in nakedness, and in the lack of all things; and He will put an iron yoke on your neck until He has destroyed you" (vv. 47–48);

· "The Lord will bring a nation against you from afar, from the end of the earth, as the eagle swoops down, a nation whose language you shall not understand" (v. 50);

· "a nation of fierce countenance who shall have no respect for the old, nor show favor to the young" (vv. 49–50);

· "Moreover, it shall eat the offspring of your herd and the produce of your ground until you are destroyed, who also leaves you no grain, new wine, or oil, nor the increase of your herd or the young of your flock until they have caused you to perish" (v. 51);

· "And it shall besiege you in all your towns until your high and fortified walls in which you trusted come down throughout your land, and it shall besiege you in all your towns throughout your land which the Lord your God has given you" (v. 52);

· "Then you shall eat the offspring of your own body, the flesh of your sons and of your daughters whom the Lord your God has given you, during the siege and the distress by which your enemy shall oppress you" (v. 53);

· "The man who is refined and very delicate among you shall be hostile toward his brother and toward the wife he cherishes and toward the rest of his children who remain, so that he will not give even one of them any of the flesh of his children which he shall eat, since he has nothing else left, during the siege and the distress by which your enemy shall oppress you in all your towns" (vv. 54–55);

· "The refined and delicate woman among you, who would not venture to set the sole of her foot on the ground for delicateness and refinement, shall be hostile toward the husband she cherishes and toward her son and daughter, and toward her afterbirth which issues from between her legs and toward her children whom she bears; for she shall eat them secretly for lack of anything else, during the siege and the distress by which your enemy shall oppress you in your towns" (vv. 56–57).

"If you are not careful to observe all the words of this law which are written in this book, to fear this honored and awesome name, the Lord your God" (v. 59),

· "then the Lord will bring extraordinary plagues on you and your descendants, even severe and lasting plagues, and miserable and chronic sicknesses" (v. 59);

· "And He will bring back on you all the diseases of Egypt of which you were afraid, and they shall cling to you" (v. 60);

· "Also every sickness and every plague which, not written in the book of this law, the Lord will bring on you until you are destroyed" (v. 61);

· "Then you shall be left few in number, whereas you were as the stars of heaven for multitude, because you did not obey the Lord your God" (v. 62);

· "And it shall come about that as the Lord delighted over you to prosper you, and multiply you, so the Lord will delight over you to make you perish and destroy you; and you shall be torn from the land where you are entering to possess it" (v. 63);

· "Moreover, the Lord will scatter you among all peoples, from one end of the earth to the other end of the earth; and there you shall serve other gods, wood and stone, which you or your fathers have not known" (v. 64);

· "And among those nations you shall find no rest, and there shall be no resting place for the sole of your foot; but there the Lord will give you a trembling heart, failing of eyes, and despair of soul" (v. 65);

· "So your life shall hang in doubt before you; and you shall be in dread night and day, and shall have no assurance of your life" (v. 66);

· "In the morning you shall say, 'Would that it were evening!' And at evening you shall say, 'Would that it were morning!' because of the dread of your heart which you dread, and for the sight of your eyes which you shall see" (v. 67);

· "And the Lord will bring you back to Egypt in ships, by the way about which I spoke to you, 'You will never see it again!' And there you shall offer yourselves for sale to your enemies as male and female slaves, but there will be no buyer" (v. 68).

Appendix E

Hesed

In the Old Testament, the word *hesed* (or *chesed*, H#2617, חֶסֶד)[1] probably sums up the character of God and illustrates the idea of a covenant more than any other word. It is used in the Old Testament 240 times. In Hebrew, the word is rich and full of meaning, but unfortunately, its meaning cannot be fully expressed when translated into English.

Hesed is translated in various translations as mercy, grace, loving-kindness, favor, steadfast love, loyalty, devotion, love, and unchanging love. Indeed, the word encompasses all of those nuances at one time. According to *Vine's Expository Dictionary of Biblical Words*,

> In general, one may identify three basic meanings of the word, which always interact: "strength," "steadfastness," and "love." Any understanding of the word that fails to suggest all three inevitably loses some of its richness. "Love" by itself easily becomes sentimentalized or universalized apart from the covenant. Yet "strength" or "steadfastness" suggests only the fulfillment of a legal or other obligation.
>
> The word refers primarily to mutual and reciprocal rights and obligations between the parties of a relationship (especially Yahweh and Israel). But hesed is not only a matter of obligation; it is also of generosity. It is not only a matter of loyalty, but also of mercy. . . . Hesed implies personal involvement and commitment in a relationship beyond the rule of law.[2]

Edmund P. Clowney says, "God sealed his love to his people by his oath. The Old Testament term is *chesed*,* and oath-bound commitment expressing freely given love. "Devotion" may be the best English translation."[3]

Chesed* is an alternate spelling of **hesed.

It should not surprise us that we do not have a word to adequately translate *hesed,* because it describes God's covenant relationship with Israel. Just as the relationship is too much to explain in a sentence, or even a chapter, the concept of covenant is too much to explain in a word.

The association of *hesed* with "covenant" keeps it from being

> misunderstood as mere providence or love for all creatures; it applies primarily to God's particular love for His chosen and covenanted people. "Covenant" also stresses the reciprocity of the relationship, but since God's *hesed* is ultimately beyond the covenant it will not ultimately be abandoned, even when the human partner is unfaithful and must be disciplined.[4]

Psalms 36:5 illustrates the difficulty of finding an adequate translation. The familiar verse is simple in construction, yet is difficult to capture the richness of meaning in translations. "Thy *lovingkindness*, O LORD, extends to the heavens, Thy faithfulness reaches to the skies." Other translations render the verse as, "Thy steadfast love," "Thy mercy," or "Thy love" "extends to the heavens." The amplified Bible says, "Your mercy and lovingkindness." All of these verses cover the aspect of love, one adds "steadfast" love, but none adequately express the strength, power, or commitment that is inherent in *hesed*.

The accounts of God's power and the steadfastness, or faithfulness, exhibited toward His chosen people are not included in the common translations.* That eliminates acknowledgement of an important part of God's relationship toward His people. For example, the God of Abraham, Isaac, and Jacob rescued Sarah and Abraham when he passed her off as his wife—twice, and brought about the birth of Isaac when Sarah was beyond child-bearing age. He rescued Moses from death as a baby and an adult, called him from a burning bush, and used him as His representative to confront Pharaoh through ten plagues, before delivering a multitude from bondage and providing for them supernaturally through forty years in the desert. He empowered a young, unknown shepherd boy to kill a giant who terrorized a whole army and raised him up to be king. God is loving and merciful, but He is also always faithful to the His covenant people. The meaning of *hesed*, includes other attributes as well.

*Unfortunately, English translators do not have an option of a word that carries all three characteristics. They are forced to make a choice that limits the understanding of **hesed**.

God's power and steadfastness (faithfulness) was unfailing—even when His people were not faithful to Him. *Hesed* includes the concepts of power and of faithfulness. Since most translations omit this concept, the church today does not see how often the Word of God alludes to the blood covenant, or to the strength and steadfastness of God.

If the concept of the blood covenant was understood by the church, the term "covenant faithfulness" might better encompass concepts of strength and steadfastness. However, it, too, is inadequate. Through the use of *hesed, we* are reminded that God's love led Him to cut a covenant, to steadfastly stand by His people even when they turned from Him, and to supernaturally use His power on their behalf.

When the full meaning of *hesed* is considered, the following verses illustrate the richness of our inheritance in covenant with the living God. They also point out how inadequate the translations are. The words representing *hesed* are in italics. You can see that each translation favors use of a particular word in the translation. For example, the King James (KJV) uses *mercy* most of the time, the New International Version (NIV) favors *love,* while the New American Standard (NAS) uses *lovingkindness*, and the English Standard Version has *steadfast love.*

As you read these verses, substitute "covenant faithfulness" and notice how the meaning deepens. Psalms uses *hesed* the most, which seems to reflect David's strong awareness of covenant and His trust in His covenant God. This is a very small sampling of the 240 times the word is used in the Bible. However, these quotes illustrate how God's children were aware of covenant through the centuries. They knew that they were God's chosen people and were in covenant with Him.

Examples of Hesed in the Bible

"O give thanks unto the Lord; for He is good: for His *mercy* endureth for ever" (Ps. 136:1 KJV).

Note: Psalms 136 recounts God's faithfulness to bring the children of Israel out of Egypt. The refrain, "For His *hesed* endures forever" is repeated in every verse, i.e., twenty-six times.

"Blessed be the Lord, the God of my master Abraham, who has not forsaken his *steadfast love* and his faithfulness toward my master. As for me, the Lord has led me in the way to the house of my master's kinsmen" (Gen. 24:27 ESV).

"In Thy *lovingkindness* Thou hast led the people whom Thou hast redeemed; in Thy strength Thou hast guided them to Thy holy habitation" (Ex. 15:13 NAS).

"And because you listen to these rules and keep and do them, the Lord your God will keep with you the covenant and the *steadfast love* that he swore to your fathers" (Deut. 7:12 ESV).

"Pardon the iniquity of this people, I pray, according to the greatness of Your *mercy*, just as You have forgiven this people, from Egypt even until now" (Num. 14:19 NKJV).

"And Solomon said, 'Thou hast shewed unto thy servant David my father great mercy, according as he walked before thee in truth, and in righteousness, and in uprightness of heart with thee; and thou hast kept for him this great *kindness*, that thou hast given him a son to sit on his throne, as *it is* this day'" (1 Kgs. 3:6 KJV).

"And hath extended *mercy* unto me before the king, and his counsellors, . . . And I was strengthened as the hand of the LORD my God *was* upon me" (Ezra 7:28 KJV).

"They refused to obey and were not mindful of the wonders that you performed among them, but they stiffened their neck and appointed a leader to return to their slavery in Egypt. But you are a God ready to forgive, gracious and merciful, slow to anger and abounding in *steadfast love*, and did not forsake them" (Neh. 9:17 ESV).

"'For the mountains may be removed and the hills may shake, but My *lovingkindness* will not be removed from you, and My covenant of peace will not be shaken,' says the LORD who has compassion on you" (Isa. 54:10 NAS).

"Thou hast granted me life and *favour*, and thy visitation hath preserved my spirit" (Job 10:12 KJV).

"'But let him who boasts boast of this, that he understands and knows Me, that I am the LORD who exercises *lovingkindness*, justice, and righteousness on earth; for I delight in these things,' declares the LORD" (Jer. 9:24 NAS).

"But, though he cause grief, he will have compassion according to the abundance of his *steadfast love*" (Lam. 3:32 ESV).

"And I prayed unto the LORD my God, and made my confession, and said, O LORD, the great and dreadful God, keeping the covenant and *mercy* to them that love him, and to them that keep his commandments" (Dan. 9:4 KJV).

"And he prayed unto the Lord, and said, I pray thee, O LORD, *was* not this my saying, when I was yet in my country? Therefore I fled before unto Tarshish: for I knew that thou art a gracious God, and merciful, slow to anger, and of *great kindness*, and repentest thee of the evil" (Jonah 4:2 KJV).

"And I will betroth you to me forever. I will betroth you to me in righteousness and in justice, in *steadfast love* and in mercy" (Hos. 2:19 ESV).

"A throne will even be established in *lovingkindness*, and a judge will sit on it in faithfulness in the tent of David; moreover, he will seek justice and be prompt in righteousness" (Isa. 16:5 NAS).

"Surely goodness and *love* will follow me all the days of my life, and I will dwell in the house of the LORD for ever" (Ps. 23:6 NIV).

"Do not remember the sins of my youth or my transgressions; according to Thy *lovingkindness* remember Thou me, for Thy goodness' sake, O Lord" (Ps. 25:7 NAS).

"All the paths of the LORD are *steadfast love* and faithfulness, for those who keep his covenant and his testimonies" (Ps. 25:10 ESV).

"I will rejoice and be glad in Thy *lovingkindness*, because Thou hast seen my affliction; Thou hast known the troubles of my soul" (Ps. 31:7 NAS).

"Many are the sorrows of the wicked; but he who trusts in the LORD, *lovingkindness* shall surround him" (Ps. 32:10 NAS).

"For you, O LORD, are good and forgiving, abounding in *steadfast love* to all who call upon you" (Ps. 86:5 ESV).

"I will sing of the *mercies* of the LORD for ever: with my mouth will I make known thy faithfulness to all generations" (Ps. 89:1 KJV).

Notes

Chapter 1

1. Trumbull, H. Clay, *The Blood Covenant*, 10–11, as quoted from Redhouse's Turkish and English Dictionaries. vv. *sood* and *soot.*
2. Trumbull, 10, 55–57.
3. Smith, Malcolm, *The Lost Secret of the New Covenant*, 11.
4. Trumbull, 57.
5. Leonard, J. E., *I Will Be Their God: Understanding the Covenant*, 10.
6. Genesis 15:6.
7. Genesis 15:8.
8. *Strong's Exhaustive Concordance*, "Hebrew" entry #4100 s. v. "mah," "maw," or "mah, mah."
9. Trumbull, 37.
10. Leonard, 26.
11. Genesis 37:19.
12. Genesis 9:4.
13. Trumbull, 38.
14. Trumbull, 41–42.
15. Genesis 21:29–33.
16. Leonard, 15.

Chapter 2

1. Genesis 12:7, 13:15–16.
2. *Strong's*, H4100, *mah*, or *ma-*, or *meh.*
3. Genesis 15:17.
4. 2 Corinthians 6:14.
5. 1 Corinthians 4:2.
6. Leviticus 5:6.
7. Leviticus 12:7.
8. Leviticus 1:3.
9. Hebrews 11:1.
10. Deuteronomy 10:16.
11. Ephesians 4:22–24, Colossians 3:9–10.
12. Genesis 15:5, 7.
13. Deuteronomy 1:21, 12:1.
14. Psalms 81:10, for example.

Chapter 3

1. Genesis 13:6–7.
2. Genesis 13:14–17.
3. Genesis 14:1–12.
4. Genesis 14:18.
5. Genesis 14:20.
6. Genesis 16:16-17:1.
7. Genesis 17.
8. Genesis 21:12–21.
9. Genesis 17:24–27.
10. *Strong's* H3327, *Yitschaq*.
11. Genesis 21:1–7.
12. Genesis 21:14–20.
13. As seen in Hebrews 11:17–19.

Chapter 4

1. Genesis 18:19
2. Deuteronomy 6.
3. Genesis 24.
4. Genesis 26:17–21.
5. Tenny, Merrel C., ed., *The Zondervan Pictorial Encyclopedia of the Bible, Vol. 1*, Grand Rapids, MI. 1975, 1976, 617.
6. Genesis 27:41–43.
7. Genesis 29:15–29.
8. The conflict: Genesis 30:25–29, 31:1–55.
9. Genesis 32:3–12.
10. Genesis 34.
11. Genesis 37−41.
12. Genesis 42–47.
13. Exodus 1:7–14.

Chapter 5

1. Exodus 1:1–3:1.
2. Tenney, 281.
3. Exodus 3:3.
4. Exodus 2:22.

5. YHWH, translated Lord, is derived from the verb HAYAH, *to be*. From NASB *Open Bible*, 1985, 56.
6. Bromiley, Geoffrey W., Gen. Editor, *The International Standard Bible Encyclopedia*, Vol. Three, Grand Rapids, MI: William B. Eerdmans Publishing Company, 1986, 418.
7. Exodus 4:14.
8. Tenney, 283.
9. Keil, C. F. and F. Delitzsch, *Commentary on the Old Testament, Vol. I*, 298.
10. Exodus 4:27.
11. Exodus 9:12; 10:1; 10:20; 11:10.
12. Exodus 7:5.
13. Exodus 4:31.
14. Exodus 7:6, 10, 20.
15. Exodus 12:35–36.
16. Exodus 13:17–21.
17. Exodus 14:13.
18. *Strong's*, H3320, *yatsab*.
19. Exodus 4:17.
20. Hebrews 13:8.

Chapter 6

1. Exodus 3:13–4:9.
2. Exodus 5:22–23.
3. *Strong's*, H3068.
4. Exodus 6:2, 5–7.
5. Exodus 7–12.
6. Exodus 4:24–26.
7. Joshua 5:5.
8. *Strong's Exhaustive Concordance*.
9. Genesis 32:24–32.
10. Exodus 7–12.
11. Exodus 14:26, 31.
12. Exodus 17:8–16.
13. Joshua 6.
14. Exodus 12 :35, Psalms 105:37.
15. Nehemiah 9:21.
16. Psalms 105:39.

17. Exodus 16:35.
18. Numbers 11:4–20.
19. Psalms 106:15.
20. Hebrews 13:8.
21. Isaiah 30:18, 1 Cor. 1:9, 1 John 1:3–4.

Chapter 7

1. *Strong's*, H2143, noun (from H2142, verb, root).
2. Exodus 17:14–16.
3. Exodus 3:15, Isaiah 12:4.
4. Joshua 8:30–35.
5. Leviticus 24:8, Exodus 20:8–11, Isaiah 56:6, and Isaiah 58:13–14.
6. Exodus 23:10–11; Leviticus 25:1–7.
7. Numbers 34-36.
8. Exodus 30:11–16.
9. Exodus 12:14; Leviticus 23.
10. Leviticus 27:30.
11. Exodus 23:32–33.
12. Exodus 40:2–35, Numbers 9:1523.
13. Numbers 9:1–14.
14. Numbers 10:11–13.
15. Psalms 78, Psalms 105.
16. Deuteronomy 27:2–6, 11–13, Joshua 8 :32–33.
17. Deuteronomy 27:1–10, Joshua 8:30–35, Genesis 15:9–18.
18. Deuteronomy 6:5.
19. Matthew 22:37–38.
20. Matthew 22:39–40.

Chapter 8

1. 1 Samuel 17:3.
2. 1 Samuel 17:11.
3. *Random House Webster's College Dictionary,* New York: Random House, 1992, "fact."
4. Ibid., "true."
5. Ibid., "truth."
6. 1 Samuel 17:34–37.
7. *Strong's*, H1697. *dabar*, daw-bawr'.
8. 1 Samuel 15:23.

Chapter 9

1. 1 Samuel 8:4–6, 19–22.
2. 1 Samuel 13:5.
3. 1 Samuel 14:27.
4. 1 Samuel 14:32–36.
5. 1 Samuel 14:36b.
6. 1 Samuel 31.
7. 1 Samuel 15:11–12.
8. 1 Samuel 24, 26.
9. Isaiah 55:9.

Chapter 10

1. 1 Samuel 13:5–15.
2. 1 Samuel 13:5.
3. 1 Samuel 14:4.
4. 1 Samuel 14:19–23.
5. 1 Samuel 14:24–26.
6. 1 Samuel 19:1.
7. See Ephesians 5:2.

Chapter 11

1. Psalms 22 :25, 28, 30–31 ; 30 :12 ; 35 :28.
2. 1 Samuel 22:9–10.
3. 2 Samuel 2:1, 5:17–25.
4. 1 Samuel 23:4.
5. 1 Samuel 24, 26.
6. 2 Samuel 7:21–24.
7. 2 Samuel 21:4–9.
8. John 1:12.

Chapter 12

1. Luke 12:27–31.
2. Exodus 14:13–14.
3. Leonard, 34. See also Deuteronomy 4:26, 30:19.
4. Isaiah 53:5, Luke 22:63–23:49.
5. Matthew 26:2, John 13:1.
6. Carlson, Messianic Rabbi Eric, "Messianic Passover Haggadah."

7. John 6:35, 51.
8. See also Mark 14:22–25; Luke 22:19–20; 1 Corinthians 11:23–26.
9. Chabad.org, http://www.chabad.org/holidays/passover/pesach_cdo/aid/504495/jewish/Why-is-Elijah-invited-in-during-the-seder.htm.
10. Matthew 16:34.

Chapter 13

1. Romans 6:23.
2. Leviticus 4:1–35, 16:1–34.
3. See Hebrews 10:19–22.
4. John 6:35, 48, 51; 1 John 1:1; John 14:6.
5. Luke 1:23.
6. *Strong's*, H4100, *pisteuo*.
7. Luke 24:49.
8. John 13:35.

Appendix A

1. Trumbull, H. Clay, *The Blood Covenant*, 37.
2. Ibid., 33.
3. Trumbull, H. Clay, *The Blood Covenant*, 34–35. Taken from *The Congo II*, 79–90, 104.

Appendix E

1. *Strong's*.
2. *Vine's*, 142
3. Clowney, Edmund P., Preaching Christ in All of Scripture, 37–38.
4. *Vine's*, 143

Bibliography

I began extensive research on the blood covenant in 1975. However, in 1996 I lost all my papers on the subject. My studies became part of me and are reflected in what I have written. I worked to acknowledge all sources, and regret if a resource from earlier years has been omitted.

Albright, Wm. F., *Archaology and the Religion of Israel.* Baltimore: The Johns Hopkins Press, 1968.

Carlson, Eric. "Messianic Passover Haggadah," "The Seder." 6. Yachatz—Breaking the Middle Matzah," http://www.zionsake.org/index.php?option=com_ content&task=view&id=66#breaking.

Chabad.org. "Why Is Elijah Invited in During the Seder," http://www.chabad.org/holidays/passover/pesach_cdo/aid/504495/jewish.

Clowney, Edmund P., *Preaching Christ in All of Scripture.* Wheaton, IL: Crossway Books, 2003.

Horton, Michael. *God of Promise: Introducing Covenant Theology.* Grand Rapids, MI: Baker Books, 2006.

Kalluveettil, Paul. *Declaration and Covenant: A Comprehensive Review of Covenant Formulae from the Old Testament and Ancient Near East.* Rome: Biblical Institute Press, 1982.

Kline, Meredith G., *By Oath Consigned.* Grand Rapids, MI: Wm B. Eerdmans Publishing Co., 1968.

Leonard, J. E., *I Will Be Their God: understanding the covenant.* Chicago: Laudemont Press, 1992.

McCarthy, D. J., *Old Testament Covenant: A Survey of Current Opinions.* Atlanta: John Knox Press. 1972.

Mendenhall, George E., *Law and Covenant in Israel and the Ancient Near East.* Pittsburgh, PA: The Presbyterian Board of Colportage of Western Pennsylvania, 1955.

Murray, Andrew. *Covenants & Blessings.* Springdale, PA: Whitaker House, 1984.

Pink, A. W., *The Divine Covenants.* Grand Rapids, MI: Baker Book House. 1973.

Random House *Webster's College Dictionary.* New York: Random House, 1992. "Why Is Elijah Invited in During the Seder," http://www.chabad.org/holidays/passover/pesach_cdo/aid/504495/jewish.

Robertson, O. Palmer. *The Christ of the Covenants*. Phillipsburg, NJ: Presbyterian and Reformed Publishing, Co., 1980.

Smith, Malcolm. "The Blood Covenant." Audiotapes of seminar taught by Malcolm Smith. Logos Tapes, 1974.

Smith, Malcolm. *The Lost Secret of the New Covenant*. Tulsa, OK, Harrison House, 2002.

Smith, Mont W., *What the Bible Says About Covenant*. Joplin, MO: College Press Publishing Company, 1981.

Smith, W. Robertson. *The Religion of the Semites: The Fundamental Institutions*. Adams and Charles Black, 1894.

Strong, James. *Strong's Exhaustive Concordance of the Bible*. Peabody, MA: Hendrickson, 1996.

Tenney, Merrill C., General Editor, *The Zondervan Encyclopedia of the Bible, Vol. Four*. Grand Rapids, MI, 1975, 1976.

Trumbull, H. Clay. *The Blood Covenant: A Primitive Rite and its Bearings on Scripture*, 2nd ed. Philadelphia: John D. Wattles. 1893. (Reprint: Kirkwood, MO: Impact Christian Books, Inc., 1975.)

Vine, W. E., Merrill F. Unger, William White, Jr., eds., *Vine's Expository Dictionary of Biblical Words: A Complete Expository Dictionary of the Old and New Testaments in One Volume*. Nashville: Thomas Nelson Publishers, 1985.

Vos, Geerhardus, *Biblical Theology: Old and New Testaments*. Grand Rapids: Wm. B. Eerdman Publishing Co., 1988.

Acknowledgements

Without the encouragement, support and help from the community around us, *The Great Exchange* would never have been written. We are especially indebted:

to the Lord, who burdened our hearts with the need for His people to learn about the ancient rite of blood covenanting, and who kept alive the dream and prayer of a someday seeing a book published.

To the Grassroots Writers Group—when Kay asked for prayer for the Lord to lead us to the author to co-write the book with us, your unanimous voice was as the voice of the Lord, when you said, "This is yours to write." Your creative criticisms and encouragement offered help and imparted energy that kept her writing.

To our EQUIP students and churches where Robert shared about the blood covenant—your enthusiasm about the message and your testimonies of increased faith and greater intimacy with God instilled in us a passion and desire to see the message spread throughout the kingdom of God. May the Lord continue to draw you close to Him.

To our children, Clay and Stephanie, Bob and Julia, Jonathan and Rebecca, and Daniel and Julia—we've seen your faith and hope grow along with ours that maybe the Lord could, indeed, use us to write a book and get it published. Thank you for always being positive, supportive, and encouraging—and for all your help with editing, computer issues, as well as website and video development. You are a blessing. We love you and are grateful for you.

To our editors, Eva Marie Everson, Alice Sullivan, Clay Camenisch, and Alicia Carman—your expertise is a gift to us and to all who read the book. Thank you for your encouragement, and the suggestions and corrections that made the book more readable.

To our God—thank you for giving us your Word and making it alive with truth for today, for your guidance and provision for the journey, and for making your strength known in our weakness. May your name be lifted up and glorified through *The Great Exchange*.

Notes

Notes

Notes

Notes

Notes

Notes

Notes

Notes